T0305908

Gender Bias in Organisations

Government and organisational policies are not enough to challenge socially constructed expectations towards gender. Arts-based methods derived from sense-making, metaphors and storytelling can support women in modifying behaviours triggered by gender stereotype threat and help them cope better in the gendered workplace.

The aim of this book is to challenge the contemporary approach of mainstreaming gender in organisations. Starting with individuals' life stories and workplace experiences to understand the common challenges for individuals and organisations, the authors review how women respond to those challenges through strategic choice and consequences both for the individual and the organisational impact. This book presents two types of arts-inspired workshops: sensory and metaphorical engagement as well as storytelling theatre.

Gender Bias in Organisations: From the Arts to Individualised Coaching discusses how gender mainstreaming initiatives have failed and proposes an individualised coaching approach based on arts-based methodology for mediating gender stereotype in the workplace. It will be of interest to researchers, academics and students in the areas of gender, work and organisation.

Dr Gillian Danby is the Owner/Managing Director of Artistry in Leadership based in the UK and is an Associate Lecturer at Northumbria University.

Dr Malgorzata Ciesielska is Associate Professor of Organisation Studies and Deputy Head of Leadership & HRM Department at Northumbria University.

Routledge Focus on Business and Management

The fields of business and management have grown exponentially as areas of research and education. This growth presents challenges for readers trying to keep up with the latest important insights. *Routledge Focus on Business and Management* presents small books on big topics and how they intersect with the world of business research.

Individually, each title in the series provides coverage of a key academic topic, whilst collectively, the series forms a comprehensive collection across the business disciplines.

Fearless Leadership
Managing Fear, Leading with Courage and Strengthening Authenticity
Morten Novrup Henriksen and Thomas Lundby

Clusters, Digital Transformation and Regional Development in Germany
Marta Götz

Gender Bias in Organisations
From the Arts to Individualised Coaching
Gillian Danby and Malgorzata Ciesielska

Entrepreneurship Development in India
Debasish Biswas and Chanchal Dey

Creating Business and Corporate Strategy
An Integrated Strategic System
Adyl Aliekperov

For more information about this series, please visit: www.routledge.com/ Routledge-Focus-on-Business-and-Management/book-series/FBM

Gender Bias in Organisations

From the Arts to Individualised Coaching

**Gillian Danby and
Malgorzata Ciesielska**

Routledge
Taylor & Francis Group

NEW YORK AND LONDON

First published 2021
by Routledge
605 Third Avenue, New York, NY 10158

and by Routledge
2 Park Square, Milton Park, Abingdon, Oxon OX14 4RN

Routledge is an imprint of the Taylor & Francis Group, an informa business

© 2021 Taylor & Francis

Library of Congress Cataloging-in-Publication Data
A catalog record for this title has been requested

ISBN: 978-0-367-86278-7 (hbk)
ISBN: 978-1-032-03891-9 (pbk)
ISBN: 978-1-003-01811-7 (ebk)

Typeset in Times New Roman
by Newgen Publishing UK

To my mum, Hanna, who taught me to be ambitious and chase my dreams.

Dr Malgorzata Ciesielska

To my parents Charles and Dorothy who encouraged me at a young age to be involved in the arts through dance, music and to engage in the theatre.

Dr Gillian Danby

They would all be very proud of our achievement in this book.

Contents

List of Figure	ix
List of Tables	x
List of Images	xi
List of Poems	xii
List of Vignettes	xiii
About the Authors	xiv
Preface	xv

1 Towards Workplace Gender Equality: An Introduction   1
1.1 Social and Economic Participation of Women 1
1.2 Potential of Arts-based Methods in Supporting Workplace Equality 4
1.3 Theories Supporting an Arts-based Methods Approach 6
    1.3.1 Sense-making 7
    1.3.2 Reflexive Practice 8
1.4 Our Arts-inspired Research Design 9
    1.4.1 Data Collection and Analysis 9
    1.4.2 Participants 10

2 Promises and Pitfalls of Gender Mainstreaming   12
2.1 Responses to Gender Inequality in the Workplace 12
    2.1.1 Policies, Systems and Processes 13
    2.1.2 Human Resource Development and Gender 14
    2.1.3 Management Theories and Practice 16
2.2 What Is Wrong with Gender Mainstreaming? 17
2.3 So What Next? 22

3 Gendered Behaviour and Career Pathways   24
3.1 The Social Construct of Gender 24
    3.1.1 Social Role Theory 26

3.2 Influences of Gendered Roles 27
    3.2.1 Education and Career Influences 28
3.3 Gender Stereotypes in the Workplace 31
    3.3.1 Gender Stereotype Threat and Its Implications 32
*3.4 Gender Stereotypes, Leadership Style and Career
    Advancement 35*
    3.4.1 Balancing Agentic and Communal Attributes 35
    3.4.2 Setting High Standards 39
    3.4.3 Early Career Influences 42
    3.4.4 Organisational Culture 43
3.5 Impact on Career Pathways 47

4 Workshops and Their Outcomes   50
4.1 Workshop Design 50
    4.1.1 Workshop One – 'Sense-making' 50
    4.1.2 Workshop Two – 'Mythodrama' 53
4.2 Insights from the Workshops and Post-workshop Interviews 56
    4.2.1 Creating a Safe Place to Explore Gender 57
    4.2.2 Self-developed Learning 59
    4.2.3 The Emotional Impact of Gendered Behaviours 61
    4.2.4 Facing the Gender Stereotype Threat 62
        4.2.4.1 Reaffirmation of Self-worth 64
        4.2.4.2 Increased Self-efficacy 67
4.3 Evaluation and Room for Improvement 71

**5 Moving Forward: Gender, Arts-Based Interventions and
    Coaching**   75
5.1 The Concept of 'Self' and 'Others' 76
5.2 From Workshops and Interviews to Coaching Interventions 78
5.3 Positive Psychology in Coaching 79
5.4 Narrative and Storytelling 81
5.5 Metaphor 83
5.6 Mindfulness and Sensory Engagement 85
5.7 Concluding Reflections 86
5.8 The Future 88

Appendix 1: Case Studies   90
Appendix 2: Glossary of Key Terms   109
References   110
Index   121

Figure

1.1   Male and female employment rates: UK, January
1971–March 2020 (ONS, 2020)   3

Tables

1.1	Key characteristics of participants	11
4.1	Structure of Workshop One: 'Sense-making'	51
4.2	Structure of Workshop Two: 'Mythodrama'	54
4.3	Themes in 'As You Like It'	54
4.4	Selected images representing emotions linked to gendered behaviours	63

Images

1   Fire extinguisher (Table 4.4)   63
2   Lock (Table 4.4)   63
3   Rubbish bins (Table 4.4)   63
4   Solitary cup on a table (Vignette 8)   64
5   An emergency exit sign (Vignette 11)   68
6   Window (Vignette 12)   69
7   Books on a shelf (Vignette 12)   70
8   Stone boulders (Case Study 2, Appendix 1)   96
9   Rubbish bins (Case Study 5, Appendix 1)   107
10   Exit sign (Case Study 5, Appendix 1)   107

Poems

1   (4.2.3)   62
2   (Case Study 1, Appendix 1)   92
3   (Case Study 2, Appendix 1)   96

Vignettes

1	Balancing Agentic and Communal Attributes	36
2	Deciding to Leave	38
3	Interpersonal Hostility and Self-doubt	38
4	Downplaying Gender	44
5	Starting to Question Working in a Male-dominated Environment	46
6	Removal of Negative Judgement of Other's	60
7	Awareness of Own Behaviours	60
8	Self-worth and New Feelings	64
9	Increased Clarity of Feelings	65
10	Increased Clarity of Own Behaviour	66
11	Increased Self-efficacy through Metaphor	67
12	Increased Self-efficacy through Sensory Engagement	69

About the Authors

Dr Gillian Danby is the Owner/Managing Director of Artistry in Leadership based in the UK and is an Associate Lecturer at Northumbria University. She has worked for many years as a senior executive in both the UK and Canada at the corporate and board levels primarily in education, social care, social housing and health services focussed on human resource management, financial management and risk management. Her most recent position was as Vice President and Chief Finance Officer at the Banff Centre for Fine Arts, Alberta, Canada. She is one of only 17% of coaches in the UK with that level of experience, and one of very few coaches who hold both a professional doctorate and coaching qualification. She is a regular contributor to a variety of international conferences as a guest speaker and workshop facilitator including the Conference Board of Canada.

Dr Malgorzata Ciesielska is Associate Professor of Organisation Studies and Deputy Head of Leadership & HRM Department at Northumbria University (UK). She is also a qualified coach and team facilitator. She has extensive work experience in a multinational environment and used to work as an expert on the United Nations and EQUAL programme – Gender Index. Her research interests range from innovation and talent management, business and professional coaching to gender issues in the workplace. She is currently involved in the research project on exploring women careers in the technology sector.

Preface

The academic journey that resulted in *Gender Bias in Organisations: From the Arts to Individualised Coaching* began years before we envisioned writing a book. In 2013, Dr Gillian (Gill) Danby, Company Director and qualified Executive Coach, initiated research on how gender affects professional women's leadership and the potential of arts-based methods to offer a solution. At that time, the idea for the doctoral research was 'a hunch'. Gill had been intrigued for many years by an awareness of her 'second nature' skills, developed in her artist training, and how she had adopted those skills in her leadership practice.

Gill's story: In late 2013, I was presented with a unique and incredible opportunity when I was offered a position at the Banff Centre for Fine Arts in Alberta, Canada, where 'the arts' had recently been incorporated into their management education programming, with reported success. I had come 'full circle', and was back where I started, in the arts. I felt compelled to explore those interests further and so 'the journey began' as I flew from Canada to the UK to meet up with Dr Malgorzata (Gosia) Ciesielska to explore 'the hunch' – the beginning of many fascinating and inspiring conversations albeit mystifying at times.

Gosia's story: I have been interested in diversity in organisations since my involvement in the United Nations Development Programme (UNDP) Gender Index in Poland back in 2005–2006. Being a woman immigrant, I have always been sensitive to the equality agenda. As a qualified coach and mentor, I have helped women in academia reach their potential. My most recent interest is in developing an understanding of how to support women's careers in male-dominated (in particular technology-related) sectors.

We (Gill and Gosia) share a social concern about the phenomenon of gender inequality in the workplace, and the absence of women reaching corporate board level, particularly in our fields of financial management and academia, and so Gosia supported Gill's research through her role as doctoral supervisor. For us, the lack of women in positions of power and authority deserved a better explanation, and more critically, we had a strong desire to develop new and practical theory to help professional women overcome the challenges they faced.

Today, many scholars and researchers share our view, as shown by the profusion of research on how gender affects leadership. We know that women who aspire to attain a leadership role will face many unexpected 'bumps in the road' – it is not as easy as travelling on a flat road. Our book offers truthful insights to the 'bumps in the road' and provides truthful insights on how to make 'the road much smoother' by cutting through *Gender Bias in Organisations: From the Arts to Individualised Coaching.*

This book writing project took shape in just over two years. From the outset of writing the proposal for this book, based on Gill's doctoral research, we have worked together – meeting regularly to share ideas, inspiration and challenges. The biggest challenge we faced was COVID-19 which in March 2020 brought our writing to an abrupt halt as we juggled with new ways of working at our university and increased responsibility for educating children and child-minding responsibilities. Simply, we lost three months of writing time, but in July 2020, we were able to pick up 'the pen', give ourselves a 'pep talk' and get 'cracking'. Our meetings now had to be 'virtual' rather than over a nice coffee or lunch, but here we are in early 2021 and we've made it. Who knows, the pandemic could be a catalyst for progress in women's equality – a topic we would love to write about in 2021.

We have worked hard to make this book interesting and accessible to readers who are not social scientists. Our aim is to share the professional women's stories in a way that is 'real' for any woman. Our belief is that all women will see themselves in the stories told. We also wanted to show the usefulness of the methods and approaches in coaching, as we both strongly believe in its importance in supporting women and men to develop their careers.

It is important to note that we are critically aware of the significant danger of individualising the impact of gender stereotype threat if this phenomenon had been the only focus of our work, but this was not our intention. We believe that organisations and societies need to reconsider their current day-to-day equality approaches and invest in support for individuals, while also investing in systemic change.

We thank the staff at Routledge for their support and our families as they encouraged us to keep going and never lose sight of our goals for this book. We would also like to give our sincere and warm thanks to the 19 women of North East England who agreed to take part in this research despite not really knowing what they were letting themselves in for. Finally, a very special thank you to Phyllida Hancock and Dr Claus Springborg who 'volunteered' to take time out of their busy schedules to facilitate the arts-based workshops. Their professionalism, experience and charisma were all truly a joy to observe.

In this book, we present insights gained from using arts-based methods in management education to explore pathways for tackling difficulties for women in the workplace, resulting from gender stereotypes. More specifically, our aim was to investigate the impact of organisational efforts in tackling gender inequality, to explore the impact of gender stereotype threat on women's leadership styles and coping strategies and to explore which arts-based methods in management education and coaching practice can moderate the impact of gender stereotype threat.

Chapter 1 provides an introduction to arts-based methods and the current state of gender equality efforts in the workplace, as well as description of our methodology.

In Chapter 2, we discuss the extent to which gender mainstreaming activities became more symbolic rather than having an actual effect. Despite political support, diversity strategies implemented in organisations have had a limited impact on gender equality in the workplace. We discuss how the current situation impacts women's careers, including the gender pay gap and issues of career progression. We illustrate these matters of concern with real-life quotes from women at various stages in their career to exemplify the failures of current gender equality policies in the workplace.

In Chapter 3, we further those arguments by discussing the extent to which gendered behaviours are evident in organisations and that professional women make strategic choices to further their careers resulting from the failure of gender mainstreaming. This chapter also contains women's real-life quotes to illustrate the strategic choices made in pursuit of their careers.

Chapter 4 presents the design and setting of the two workshops and how they were carried out. Workshop One – 'Sense-making' was primarily an individualistic approach, and subject matter centred, with each participant focussed on their own individual issue. Workshop Two – 'Mythodrama' was a more collaborative approach, primarily in the form of group work, and at times was facilitator directed, for example, in the presentation of particular leadership theories.

Chapter 5 demonstrates that the vicious circle of gender stereotype fulfilment and propagation set in motion by gender stereotype activation can be broken through an individualised arts-based coaching approach. We strongly believe that this approach can moderate gender stereotype threat by increasing women's positive self-view and self-belief and thus provide a perspective that gives professional women the opportunity to address the organisational realities they face at any given time adequately.

In Appendix 1, we have included five case studies of professional women and the impact of gender stereotypes on their life and career path. The cases are narrated around the individual, their background, education and career and how they were affected by gender stereotypes, gender interventions and the research workshop. We have also posed reflective questions to assist readers in their learning.

Appendix 2 contains a glossary of key terms used in this book and their definitions.

1 Towards Workplace Gender Equality

An Introduction

Gender stereotypes are a generalised view or a preconception about the attributes and characteristics of a particular group. In the case of this study, those specific groups are women professionals and leaders. Gender stereotype threat is the fear that a person's behaviour may confirm an existing stereotype of a group with which that person identifies, which can negatively impact an individual's behaviour. This book investigates the potential of arts-based methods in management education to moderate the impact of gender stereotype threat for women. Gender in organisations is a mature field that has been given much attention over the past 30 years. Meanwhile, arts-based approaches in management education are an adolescent field that has gained momentum since the early 2000s. The literature in both fields is extensive, and specifically, there is an ever-growing interest in the impact of gender stereotypic behaviour in the workplace (Eagly and Heilman, 2016) and the untapped potential of arts-based methods (Sutherland and Jelinek, 2015). Further, Roberts and Creary (2013) suggested that navigating 'the self' is critical for working in a diverse world and can actively engage individuals in shaping, and sustaining their own identity, which may serve well to challenge the complexities in a gendered work environment. This notion is a good fit with arts-based learning that revolves around emotional and subjective outcomes with the potential to influence the current dominant pedagogy in management education.

In the introduction to this book, we draw on the existing data and studies of the social and economic participation of women, gender in the workplace and the failure to deliver gender equality.

1.1 Social and Economic Participation of Women

The norms governing women's social and economic participation have changed over the past 30 years. One of the key developments in the

UK was the introduction of the Equal Pay Act (1970), prohibiting any less favourable treatment of men and women in terms of pay; the Sex Discrimination Act (1975), promoting equality of opportunity between men and women; the Employment Protection Act (1975), making it illegal to sack a women due to pregnancy; the lone parent income support changes (2008), which changed conditions for lone parent income support; and the changes to women's state pension age (2010), which increased the number of women working past 60 (Institute for Fiscal Studies, 2018). Further, the last 30 years has seen dramatic and important changes in the world of work in the form of globalisation, workplace and society, including increased competitive pressures, disruptive technologies and greater social, ecological and sustainability consciousness (Christensen et al., 2018; Purvis et al., 2018). Significant changes in the workplace include a global shift from a manufacturing-based economy to an information- and service-based one, benefitting women's employment in management positions, by increasing the value of 'brain power' over 'muscle power'; organisations' desire for a competitive advantage by mapping employees to their customer base; and more women in full-time higher education leading to more women being available for management positions (Powell, 1999).

Over the same period, the intersection between work and family life has also changed allowing more women to work, for example, women choosing to remain single, defer marriage or have 'house husbands' (Hurn, 2013); freedom of choice in reproduction (Powell, 1999); more organisations introducing programmes to support family or caring needs (Hurn, 2013); lower fertility rates (Adsera, 2004); and an increase in single-parent households fuelled by higher divorce rates (OECD, 2011). These changes have all contributed to an increase in the numbers of women employed in the UK. This meteoric rise led to an increase in female employment rates, which reached a record high at 72% in 2020, illustrated in Figure 1.1. However, it should be noted that the increase is partly due to changes in the state pension age for women. Women retiring at older age will mean that the overall number of women in the workforce will increase.

The UK employment rate, the proportion of people aged 16 to 64 years who are in employment, for men was 78.6% in July–September 2020, indicating that the gap between the employment rate for men and women was about 6.6 percentage points, which represents the smallest gap in this indicator since comparable records began in 1971 (Office for National Statistics [ONS], 2020). Furthermore, in 2019, 40% of women in employment were working part-time, compared to 13% of men (House of Commons Library, 2020), and 54.7% of women reported

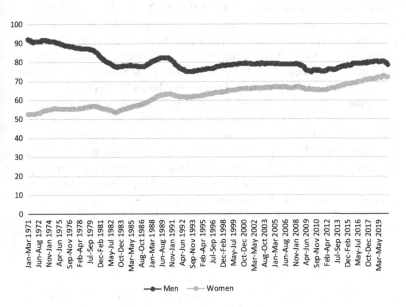

Figure 1.1 Male and female employment rates: UK, January 1971–March 2020 (ONS, 2020).

working on 'zero hours contracts' (a contract with no guaranteed minimum hours). In addition, it should be noted that 66% of people on 'zero hours contracts' are working part-time, compared to 25.3% of people in employment who are not on zero hours contracts (ONS, 2018b).

Furthermore, there remains a gender pay gap for full-time workers, which is entirely in favour of men in all occupations, with the smallest gender pay gap having almost equal employment shares between men and women. Holding all other factors constant, for 2017 women's pay growth in respect of age was lower than men's pay growth and also stopped growing at a younger age. From age 40 onwards, the gap widens reaching its peak between the ages of 50 and 59 (ONS, 2018a). The gender pay gap among all employees in the UK was 15.5% in 2020 (ONS, 2020).

Despite the increase in female employment rates, the proportion of women in managerial and senior positions is reportedly modest across all sectors. In 'public life', the proportion of women in managerial and senior positions increased from 31% in 2001 to 35% in 2016 (House of Commons Library, 2018). This proportion is, however, 23.6% for managers, directors and senior officials, as defined in the Standard

Occupational Classification (SOC) (ONS, 2010). The percentage of women managers remains higher in 'traditional' female sectors – for example, health and social services and human resources (House of Commons Library, 2018). Data show that women's representation on the Financial Times Stock Exchange (FTSE) 100 boards has risen from 11% in 2007 to 28.6% in 2019 (Hampton-Alexander Review, 2019).

Women are outnumbered by men in leadership positions in the neighbouring European Union's (EU) corporate sector. On average, only 23.3% of board members of the largest publicly listed companies in the EU are women. This represents an increase from 11.9% in 2010 when the EU first put the issue of women in leadership positions high on the political agenda. However, there is still considerable progress to be achieved if gender balance is to be attained (European Commission, 2016).

The above dramatic and important changes in the workforce have focussed researchers and theorists on the many benefits that women could bring to the workplace. Firstly, gender diversity enables improved financial performance and organisational credibility (Perrault, 2015). Secondly, improved governance and ethics result from enriched decision-making (Watson, 2015). Thirdly, female talent can be leveraged by increasing the understanding of gender policy issues through more prevalence of female role models (Terjesen et al., 2014). Finally, improved ratings for corporate social responsibility can be achieved (Bear et al., 2010). The balance of evidence from the literature concludes that gender diversity is required for more fundamental reasons other than organisational performance alone, suggesting a broader duty towards various stakeholders and moral imperative for building equal society for everyone. Furthermore, greater diversity signals to stakeholders that the organisation pays attention to women and minorities, being socially responsible which results in enhanced corporate reputations and potentially positively impacting on performance.

1.2 Potential of Arts-based Methods in Supporting Workplace Equality

The data quoted above show that the efforts of governments and organisations to address gender inequality in the workplace have achieved only symbolic (Lee-Gosselin et al., 2013), but tokenistic, results. Gendered behaviours are passively developed in childhood and adolescence from the observation of social norms (Marcus and Harper, 2014). This social enculturation establishes and teaches individuals the accepted norms and values of the culture of society as well as its accepted behaviour. In response to gendered behaviours in the workplace, the literature reports that leader characteristics are changing to incorporate both male and female qualities (Berkery et al., 2013). However, violating acceptable gender norms can have a significant impact on work–life harmony, as women attempt to deal with the various challenges in today's organisations. In this respect, women are also affected by other cultural factors that create a labyrinth of numerous barriers, such as household and childcare responsibilities. Scientific research that appears to have given attention to studies that fit prevailing cultural norms (Eagly and Heilman, 2016) – thus discouraging studies that can reveal the true complexity and consequences of gender from those most significantly impacted – is causing growing unease among authors and researchers. Furthermore, management education programmes have not adequately tackled gendered issues in the workplace (Kelan and Dunkley Jones, 2010), as leadership is generally presented as being gender neutral and culturally neutral. As such, leadership theorists have failed to acknowledge the impact of those factors, including gender stereotypes, which, in turn, has created problems in the development of tomorrow's leaders, who need to understand their own preferred styles and behaviours, and how these may differ from those preferred by others (Eagly and Chin, 2010). Therefore, this study adopts an unconventional kind of management education, an arts-based approach to provide a broader humanistic perspective and prepare women leaders to cope with behaviours associated with gender stereotypes, which potentially hinder career aspirations and/or career progression.

Social scientists concur that using arts-based methods in management learning provides an opportunity to explore the aesthetic sphere affording alternative ways for leaders to make sense of increasing complexities beyond the boundaries of scientific methods and analytical reasoning (Adler, 2006). Aesthetics comes from aisthetikos whose Greek meaning is 'sense perception'. Barnard (1938) described five key elements of aesthetics: 'feeling' (showing emotion or sensitivity), 'judgement' (the ability to come to sensible conclusions), 'sense' (sight, smell, hearing, taste, touch), 'proportion and balance' (equilibrium in judgement) and 'appropriateness' (fit for purpose). Many researchers agree that aesthetics presents fertile ground for experiential learning, innovation, creation and improvisation (Koivunen and Wennes, 2011; Sutherland and Jelinek, 2015) that lead to an 'intelligence of feeling' as described by Witkin (2009, p. 59). Aesthetics and the arts have comparable qualities which have been understood for many years:

> abstract art frees our brain from the dominance of reality, enabling it to flow within its inner states, create new emotional and cognitive

associations, and activate brain-states that are otherwise harder to access.

(Aviv, 2014, p.1)

These behaviours of compassion, understanding and feeling are described by Sutherland (2012, p. 26) as 'the soft issues of managing and leading'. Social scientists agree that using arts-based methods in management education provides an opportunity to explore the aesthetic sphere, thus affording alternative ways for leaders to make sense of increasing complexities beyond the boundaries of scientific methods and analytical reasoning. This aspect, in turn, affords the transformation of the experiences through the development of non-rational or non-logical capabilities in a personified way to cultivate human potential and experiential knowing (Springborg and Sutherland, 2015; Springborg and Ladkin, 2018).

1.3 Theories Supporting an Arts-based Methods Approach

Arts-based methods flow from the underlying assumption that such methods can make important information available for sense-making and reflection (Springborg, 2010), which can have a profound impact on an individuals' understanding of an experience or situation (Taylor and Ladkin, 2009). Further, traditional, rational-orientated means of doing education are recognised as not meeting the challenges found in organisations today (Adler, 2011; Edwards et al., 2013), and that the wider adoption of experiential learning methods in executive education and leadership development could be beneficial (Weick, 1998; Kolb and Kolb, 2008). According to some scholars, management education programmes have not adequately tackled gendered issues in the workplace, with the education of business leaders continuing to be based on a masculine model (Kelan and Dunkley Jones, 2010; Ely et al., 2011). In turn, this issue has created problems in the development of tomorrow's leaders, as individual leaders need to understand their own preferred style and behaviours, and how these may differ from those preferred by others (Chin and Sanchez-Hucles, 2007).

In arts-based methods, the experiential path is critical, as the intersection of engaged participation, and making connections between the arts-based event, and oneself occur (Sutherland and Jelinek, 2015), with the end product being 'aesthetic knowing' (Hanson et al., 2007). In this approach to management learning, connections arise through three interlinked ideas: sense-making processes (Weick et al., 2005); reflective activities (Gray, 2007; Cunliffe, 2009b) influenced by consideration of 'self' and 'others' (Holt and Macpherson, 2010), which are discussed further in the following sections.

1.3.1 Sense-making

Sense-making activities involve inquiring into and thus interpreting an individual's sense of belonging and fit within a social context to derive meaning from challenging situations and to reconstruct a positive sense of self. Essentially, 'when people engage in sensemaking, they impose abstractions and categories that mean they move farther and farther away from their initial impressions' (Weick, 2007, p. 12).

Paying attention to our senses ensures the ongoing process of sense-making that creates personal experience, which is second nature to artists, who view this process from the perspective of something that is sensed, not something that is calculated (Springborg, 2010). For example, paintings bring attention to something previously unnoticed, and through theatre, attention is directed to unnoticed aspects of life, achieved by taking a distance from reality. Direct sensory experiences can be described as a tacit form of knowing, where experiences encourage meaning-making related directly to personal experiences as part of the human system, rather than an organisational issue thereby 'enacting one's true self' (Ladkin and Taylor, 2010, p. 72). Indeed, as Weick (2007, p. 15) himself observes, 'all of these non-logical activities enable people to solve problems and enact their potential'.

The primary motives of sense-making are (i) to make sense and reflect on the difficulties experienced in career progression (Roberts and Creary, 2013) and (ii) to bridge the gap between old and new roles and identities (Ibarra and Barbulescu, 2010). Sense-making, therefore, involves activities of inquiring and interpreting one's embeddedness within a social context that helps individuals derive meaning from challenging situations and reconstruct a positive sense of self.

Many authors highlight the value of considering sensory experiences, placing a significant importance on spending time with the experience, without reflecting upon it, or in drawing conclusions from it. These scholars refer to this aspect using Heidegger's concept of dwelling (Wicks and Rippon, 2010; Sutherland, 2012) or using explanatory phrases, such as 'staying with the senses' (Springborg, 2010). Seeley and Reason (2008), drawing a parallel between the ability to 'hang out' in uncertainty, without trying to use the mind to reach certainty, argue that reflecting too quickly will interrupt the intellect. This approach is an act of allowing an impulse (or impulses) to come in, a form of 'open' attentiveness that offers the phenomenon a chance to state its own gesticulation, and such holding back requires discipline, which, as such, may offer the potential to remove the vulnerability of stereotype threat.

1.3.2 Reflexive Practice

Reflexive practice stems from the roots of critical theory and has been discussed by social scientists for over 30 years, influenced in the main by feminist researchers and those from hermeneutic and critical theory traditions (Gray, 2009). Reflexivity is about questioning one's own taken-for-granted assumptions as opposed to reflexive practice which is reflecting on actions and is a continuous process of learning.

In more recent years, reflexivity has become a focus of management and leadership development (Gray, 2007) and, according to Cunliffe (2009b, p. 406), is fundamental to management learning because it is about 'who we are, how we relate to others, and what we do – and that is why reflexivity is a cornerstone for ethical and responsive management'. Therefore, by engaging with the arts, it enables us 'to draw upon, and subsequently reflect on, a deep well of unconscious stuff' (Taylor and Ladkin, 2009, p. 58). The unconscious aspects may be unexamined suppositions that the individual operates from (Springborg and Sutherland, 2015) or even that organisations operate from. In using reflexive practices, practitioners are particularly concerned with unsettling and questioning notions of social realities, or those developed from experience of those realities, and whether we can explain social realities accurately and with neutrality. Fundamentally, it is recognising the role we play with others in shaping our social and organisational realities (Cunliffe, 2009a): for example, gender stereotypes. Drawing on social constructionist suppositions reflexivity involves questioning existing experiences rather than the reflexive questioning of ideologies, texts or theories. A questioning of self rather than others means 'shifting our assumptions from learning from an epistemological (learning about theories and techniques that can be applied to practice) to an ontological perspective involving learning within experience' (Cunliffe and Easterby-Smith, 2004, p. 35).

Reflexivity enables possibilities for change in everyday interaction, and 'little by little, this can undermine the structures and practices of domination' (Cunliffe, 2002, p. 37). In essence, by focussing on experiences, change may occur from within, through recognition of one's own place and the ability to shape knowledge, learning and organisational realities. As Weick et al. (2005) argue in relation to sense-making, individuals engage in situating activity to develop who they are, their knowledge of self within specific contexts.

1.4 Our Arts-inspired Research Design

The empirical material in this book comes from a qualitative and inductive study (Ciesielska and Jemielniak, 2018). Data were gathered from pre-workshop life-grid development interviews, observation of two separate arts-based workshops and post-workshop interviews. The fieldwork was conducted between January and May 2017 in the North East of England. Northern England has a strong manufacturing and energy base, which has led to a predominantly male-dominated working culture. Northern women are stereotyped as strong-willed and independent, and there is a tradition of matriarchal families, where the woman of the house runs the home and controls the family's finances.

1.4.1 Data Collection and Analysis

It was important to situate both cultural and historical personal experiences within the discourses of this study. As such, the first step was retrospective data capture in the form of life-grid development to facilitate recall to a range of events and experiences in the research area across time spans (Brannen and Nilsen, 2011). According to Powell (1999, p. 345): 'gender effects should not be considered in isolation from the effects of the wide range of personal characteristics that may influence people's sense of identity'. Biographical data were also needed to interrogate some of the assumptions underpinning the previous research into the role that gender plays in disadvantaging women in a career progression context. Data from this step were primarily used in Chapter 3.

The second step was non-participant observation which gave us an opportunity to observe the curriculum at work, and record the action as it was taking place, providing a further source of data, and to support post-workshop interviews (Ciesielska et al., 2018). We invited two experienced facilitators to design and run a one-day workshop each. Both workshops concentrated on gender issues in the workplace and involved arts-based methods. Participants worked with metaphors and sensory experience in Workshop One and with Shakespeare's play 'As You Like It' in Workshop Two. The fundamental value of this approach was to enhance intellectual creativity, open new viewpoints and challenge how things are done, facilitating sense-making and reflexive practice. The third step was post-workshop interviews to elicit stories about events, behaviours and beliefs in relation to the topics discussed, both during the workshop and in post-workshop dialogue, in a 'non-directive' manner (Saunders et al., 2012). Data collected through observation and post-workshop interviews were primarily used in Chapter 4.

The narratives provided powerful insights into women's career choices and career development experiences, their leadership styles and the day-to-day realities of gendered behaviours in the workplace, rather than focussing on women's traits, and detaching the research from the circumstances surrounding their work, as in the current literature. Exploring notions of 'self' through arts-based methods enabled individuals' to draw upon and reflect on unconscious thinking relating to gender stereotype threat. This more sensate approach provided a forum for participants to challenge issues important to them, creating space to reflect on internalised gender stereotypes and their impact.

Data were analysed using thematic analysis (King et al., 2018). This study brought a sophisticated understanding to the research topic by focussing on the lived gender experiences and social relations of 19 women with a broad range of key characteristics including management level from novice to experienced and an age range from 21 to 63 years.

1.4.2 Participants

The informants were identified to enable the exploration of the gender stereotype threat behaviour in a workplace setting (Gray, 2009), through 'rich cases', studied in depth (Patton, 2002). A purposeful, maximum variation sampling strategy was adopted. Recruitment of informants took place in our own locality in the North East of England. Snowball sampling was used to identify volunteer informants from personal networks of individuals who have a special interest in the field of study, for example, women's networking groups, work colleagues, artistic field contacts, business ties, academic contacts and social networks. Those initial informants then identified subsequent informants. In this way, we were able to identify and gain access to a wider potential sample (Cassell and Symon, 1994). Through an initial conversation with potential informants, maximum variation sampling was used subjectively to ensure as wide a variation as possible. Final informants were chosen based on offering a broad range of key characteristics at the time of data collection, illustrated in Table 1.1. This approach allowed for the development of rich picture information regarding how individuals' view the gender challenges in their field of activity, to bring a

Table 1.1 Key characteristics of participants

Occupations	
Community services	1
Teaching and learning	3
General management	8
Sales	1
Social work	1
Personnel and organisational development	1
Research	1
Policy and strategic planning	2
Consultant	1
Employment sectors	
Local government	3
Service sector	2
Health care	1
Education	4
Construction	1
Fire service	4
Housing and community care	4
Organisational levels	
Director level	3
Senior management team/department head	7
Senior managers	4
Middle management/professional staff	5
Organisation type	
Female-dominated environment	5
Male-dominated environment	5
Mixed environment	9
Age (years)	
20–29	2
30–39	3
40–49	6
50–59	7
Over 60	1
Life situation	
Single or divorced	5
Single or divorced – with younger children	2
Married or partnered	6
Married or partnered – with dependent children	6

sophisticated understanding to the topic, reducing the likelihood of a homogeneous sample (Lee, 2000). A total of 20 women participants were selected, but 1 opted out before the workshop took place, leaving us with 19 participants in total.

2 Promises and Pitfalls of Gender Mainstreaming

In this chapter, we discuss the extent to which gender mainstreaming has been implemented in organisations and its impact on gender equality in the workplace. We argue that despite the political and strategic nature of gender mainstreaming activities, they are more symbolic rather than having an actual effect on women's careers. The recent data from national and international surveys highlight the perpetuating pay gap and issues around career progression.

Before we move on, it should be noted that in this research, the participants were recruited through personal networks. To ensure anonymity, the real names of participants were changed to pseudonyms, and each was assigned a 'professional number'. We have included real-life quotes of women at various stages of their careers to illustrate the failures of current gender equality policies in the workplace.

2.1 Responses to Gender Inequality in the Workplace

Gender mainstreaming was developed following criticism of various early 1970s initiatives that emphasised the inclusion of women in organisational development. The criticism centred on the lack of acknowledgement of social gender relations and a critique of dominant development paradigms (Mahapatro, 2014). For example, the nature of women's interpersonal subordination was disregarded, and gender power relations remained intact (Mukhopadhyay, 2014). Gender mainstreaming is associated with the United Nations (UN) Economic and Social Council meeting (1995) held in Beijing. Most organisations adhere closely to the definition set out in Beijing:

> Mainstreaming a gender perspective is the process of assessing the implications for women and men of any planned action, including legislation, policies or programmes, in all areas and at all levels.

It is a strategy for making women's as well as men's concerns and experiences an integral dimension of the design, implementation, monitoring and evaluation of policies and programmes in all political, economic and societal spheres so that women and men benefit equally and inequality is not perpetuated. The ultimate goal was to achieve gender equality.

The idea of gender mainstreaming was and still is that organisations' policymaking and decision-making processes themselves are gendered, implying that gender equality can be achieved by incorporating a gender perspective at all levels of policymaking (Davids et al., 2014). Many organisations, researchers and academics (e.g. Alston, 2014) recognise that this approach oversimplifies the phenomenon of gender inequality, as the statement incorporated an assumption that the world prior to gender mainstreaming was unbiased (Davids et al., 2014). This assumption places the agenda into two specific areas: (i) the overhaul of policymaking and (ii) societal transformation. The recognition of two areas represents a difference between how gender equality was initially conceived and how it is now understood. Mainstreaming is not only about gender concerns in policies and programmes but also gender issues within organisations. It is thus acknowledged that organisations themselves are gendered and that this gendering of organisations is related to their similarly gendered outcomes (Alston, 2014).

2.1.1 Policies, Systems and Processes

The pressure to achieve measurable results in the UK has encouraged a focus on technical solutions with an array of analytical tools including checklists, gender impact assessments, awareness raising, training manuals, expert meetings and data collection that have contributed to and reinforced the belief that gender equality could be both achieved and measured (de Waal, 2006). The review of existing policies and the development of new policies are intended to ensure that those policies do not support gender stereotyping or gender bias. Often the promotion of images of diverse individuals on career sites, websites and any social networks, particularly relating to recruitment, accompanies this type of intervention, for example, images that challenge gender stereotypes. Other policy changes include minimising the awareness of gender in recruitment processes, for example, ensuring that the names and potentially other demographic information are not visible to those analysing applications, ensuring a gender balance on recruitment panels, evaluation of all candidates against an agreed set of criteria, support to workplace flexibility, parental leave policies and the adoption of whistle-blowing policies (Lee-Gosselin et al., 2013; Parpart, 2014). Furthermore, to ensure the visibility of their commitment to gender equality and to claim an element of progression, many organisations apply for numerous awards. However, some argue that despite an increasingly sophisticated stock of analytical tools and gender experts, the transformative potential of gender equality remains in question (Alston, 2014), with policy separated from practice, and because 'gender' has become a substitute for 'women', with a promise of inclusion rather than transformation (Parpart, 2014).

2.1.2 Human Resource Development and Gender

Over recent years, organisations have moved from identifying training needs to identifying learning needs – the implication being that development is owned by the learner with the need, rather than the trainer, seeking to satisfy that need (Torrington et al., 2009). This approach has implications for who identifies the needs and the way that those needs are met. Many organisations have responded with a partnership approach between the individual and organisation, whereby individuals are encouraged to take responsibility and ownership for their development (ibid). Cureton and Stewart (2014) note that the most obvious change has seen the word 'training' being replaced by 'learning', and that learning is often done 'on-the-job'. This change places much of the learning in a gendered environment with the probability of perpetuating gendered behaviours and attitudes, rather than achieving the desired transformation, facilitated by creative and innovative solutions. Coaching and mentoring are becoming a leading form of workplace and professional development (CIPD, 2015) and are mostly used for increasing leadership, performance, and to facilitate promotion but rarely for diversity.

Two definitions of human resource development are suggested by Gold et al. (2013): (i) organised learning experiences provided by employers, within a specific period, to bring about the possibility of performance improvement and/or personal growth and (ii) planned interventions in organisational and individual learning processes. The former focusses on employers, whereas the latter allows for a broader context. Organisational gender training typically falls into the latter as part of an overarching strategy and a process of organisational change towards greater equality (Lombardo and Mergaert, 2013). The notion that gender mainstreaming is related to organisational transformation is supported by many (Benschop et al., 2012), but what is to be transformed is unclear. Some feminists understand gender mainstreaming in terms of the transformation of dominant powers, whereas others associate gender mainstreaming with the transformation of social gender relations or relating it to the transformation of institutional structures of government and the state (Mukhopadhyay et al., 2006). Responding to the lack of focus on the gender of social change in organisational development methodologies, many researchers have discussed change programmes and interventions targeted at gender equality in organisations. Generally, those researchers are critical of, or even sceptical about, the possibility of change, focussing on the perseverance and resilience of inequalities, emphasising the partiality and incompleteness of the changes realised (Benschop et al., 2012).

A dynamic for 'real' change will only arise when the cultural aspects are transformed within an organisation (Mahapatro, 2014; Mukhopadhyay, 2014), meaning a decrease in gender stereotypic behaviour and demonstrable commitment from the top to equality. There are many barriers to organisational change, and gender is no exception, as genuine organisational change is complex, difficult and problematic, no matter what the specific subject is. Lombardo and Mergaert (2013) suggest that resistance is more likely to be prevalent in gender training, as the change challenges the norms, practices and assumptions concerning the relations between women and men who work at the level of individual and organisational actors. Many scholars agree (Parpart, 2014; van Eerdewijk and Davids, 2014), suggesting that resistance to change is likely to appear when the existing organisational culture, norms, beliefs, attitudes and values are affected by the change efforts. It is argued that gender training provokes reflections about people's own gender roles and their stereotypes, sometimes making them feel exposed to criticism or suggesting a need for changes in their own personal identity (Lombardo and Mergaert, 2013). This questioning of the personal sphere can trigger reactions of fear and self-protection that can move people to develop attitudes of resistance to such activities. These reactions can result in the importance of gender equality being trivialised and minimalised and also a refusal to accept responsibility for dealing with gender equality issues (ibid). In their exploration of resistance to gender training, Lombardo and Mergaert (2013) identified that resistance to change falls into three forms: (i) denial of the need for gender change – 'equality is fantasy', 'disbelief about gender data', 'defending traditional gender roles as natural'; (ii) trivialising gender equality – 'it's not relevant to our work', 'time will fix the problem', 'the issue is too complex', 'gender equality is a problem for women not men' and (iii) refusing to accept responsibility – 'gender inequality only concerns other cultures, not us'. These findings concur with Eagly and Chin's (2010) claim that many organisations have recognised the individual contributions of men and women, presenting leadership as a phenomenon that is primarily gender and culture neutral. Hence, those involved in training have failed to acknowledge the impact of those factors, which has created problems in the development of individual leaders who need to understand their own preferred style and behaviours and how these may differ from those preferred by others (Chin and Sanchez-Hucles, 2007). It is reported that resistance to change manifests itself in some form of misinterpretation of the approach by people within organisations, notably the senior management teams (Lee-Gosselin et al., 2013).

The pivotal role of Chief Executive Officers (CEOs) and executive committees in driving organisational change is generally accepted, but a debate remains about who leads the gender equality change process, given that how power operates in an organisation, and how change takes place, differ substantially (Davids et al., 2014). The gender of the leader inescapably impacts the gender change intervention in that gendered expectations and choices position men as powerful and effective champions. According to de Vries (2015), to ignore this aspect would lead to 'power blindness' and could be harmful to the organisation because the men leading the change could become 'gender change heroes', thereby strengthening the gendered status quo. Furthermore, Mukhopadhyay et al. (2006) maintain that no matter how much leadership comes from 'the top', change has its limits, particularly when it has to occur with the leaders and decision-makers themselves. This aspect seems particularly true where gender equality is concerned, with practices, ideas or behaviours that perpetuate gender inequity, as they are especially resistant to change. Beschop et al. (2012) agree, maintaining that the approach needs to be transformative and aimed at changing gender as a structure, everyday organisational routines and interactions, thereby bringing an end to the production of gender inequalities. Indeed, it is imperative that organisations 'contend with the reality of institutional power' (Mukhopadhyay, 2014, p. 365).

2.1.3 Management Theories and Practice

In an organisational context, management theories are related to explicit management knowledge derived from the documented experiences of practising managers and the use of empirical data to derive principles, frameworks and tools. Management practice, on the other hand, refers to a range of activities carried out by 'managers' of organisations

(Cole and Kelly, 2015). Over the years, elements of management have remained consistent. However, external environment influences have changed expectations in the workplace and the marketplace: for example, the social and economic participation of women in work and an expectation that employees are mapped to the organisational customer base. To this end, 'change' in both the external and internal environments is a common feature and a challenge faced by managers which, in turn, demands creative ideas and solutions to business needs (Cole and Kelly, 2015). In considering those managerial demands, Child (1997) introduced the notion of strategic choice theory, whereby power-holders within organisations decide upon courses of strategic action. The decisions of the power-holders are impacted by their values, attitudes and beliefs, including culture, life experiences and perceptions based on the social construct of gender. These life experiences impact evaluations, thoughts and mental processes, and therefore, choices and actions are based on how individuals perceive the world and how they should operate within it. In other words, managers filter everything through their individual world view and assign meaning to the people, things and events of their lives, based on personal interpretation within the context of their environment. Management theory prescribes what managers and leaders should be and do, but the reality is often messy, influenced by gender stereotypes, leading to inconsistencies with theory (Cole and Kelly, 2015).

Governments and organisations have developed and implemented many initiatives within the context of new management practices in response to gender inequality, with initiatives generally led by human resource managers, and typically incorporating gender targets and quotas (Vinnicombe et al., 2015); human resources development programmes including diversity training (Kalinoski et al., 2013) and the introduction and review of policies, systems and processes (Lee-Gosselin et al., 2013; Parpart, 2014). The focus of initiatives may be exclusively on women, on both men and women, or on men only, and are generally designed to promote exchange between different groups and to facilitate career development for those who have lagged behind (Dobbin and Kalev, 2013) and to help individuals work together in a diverse workforce.

2.2 What Is Wrong with Gender Mainstreaming?

Not surprisingly, and concurring with the findings of others, we found that gender stereotypical behaviours are dominant in organisational relationships and processes across many employment sectors. These conscious – and often unconscious – processes are shaping the nature and culture of organisations, and this re-creation of shared systems of meaning is exhibited by both men and women, thereby hampering gender mainstreaming efforts, hence inhibiting 'true' organisational change.

Sixteen of the nineteen women participating in our study confirmed that organisational training specifically aimed at addressing gender issues is virtually non-existent: '*I can't recall any specific diversity awareness training in terms of male, or female*' [Professional 17]. Indeed, many confirm an organisational belief that 'expert' meetings, in the form of gender networks or diversity groups, can move the agenda forward. Membership of such groups generally consists of organisational champions, who have a strong commitment to gender equality but who are also woefully under-resourced, as illustrated by Linda:

> *I'm really passionate and dead interested in that* [referring to the gender network]. *I'm having to be careful that it doesn't take over. It would be a full time job, and I've got my day job as well. Really, really passionate at the moment about the gender issues, as we have a long way to go.*
>
> [Professional 14]

This finding is also consistent with other scholars (e.g. Mahapatro, 2014) who confirmed that the implementation of gender mainstreaming has not been consistent with the prescriptions of theorists and practitioners.

We found that the use of 'technical' tools was particularly evident in the public sector, where participants portrayed inclusion rather than transformation (for example, in the regular 'presentation' of women to appease an external assessor):

> *We're not perfect by any stretch of the imagination, and no matter how many glass dishes or glass plates or trophies you have, it doesn't change what happens on a day-to-day basis.*
>
> [Professional 12]

One woman described how she is 'wheeled out', clearly tokenism, for every external assessment, as one of the few women holding a senior position in her male-dominated environment:

> *Every assessment and audit I was actually pushed to the front, [...]. I am happy to speak positively about the organisation, but I think that went against my values because we should be being transparent.*

People were doing it for the right reasons – quality assessments or whatever audit. But now 10 years later I'm still the only female. Not against my principles, but it's got a bit old. Oh yes, let's tick the box.

[Professional 14]

Going further, there was also evidence of resistance to change within the narratives concurring with Lombardo and Mergaert (2013) that the required change challenges relationship norms, provokes reflection, triggering fear and self-protection – thereby leading to resistance. Consistent with Parpart (2014), Linda's narrative about a difficult situation with a senior male manager also confirmed that seeking a solution to openly discriminatory behaviour is difficult, and the response to a gender issue being raised can propagate the discriminatory behaviour and often leads to exasperation:

I did take advice from the Senior HR Manager who said 'well just go off on the sick' and I said 'I'm not sick, I don't want to do that, I just want to get out of this situation'. That was a terrible time. The HR manager described him as a trail of destruction, it was quite frustrating [as no one wanted to deal with it].

[Professional 14]

Most participants were married or in a domestic partnership, and many had caring responsibilities. They portrayed a strong belief that organisational policies aimed at supporting families were ineffective and were subject to gendered beliefs, described by Cole and Kelly (2015) as the 'messiness' of management reality and inconsistency with management theory and practice. This finding is supported by Child's (1997) strategic choice theory which indicates that the decisions of the power-holders are impacted by their gendered values, attitudes and beliefs. For example, we found that women (and men) frowned upon individuals taking advantage of flexible working policies. Consistent with Lee-Gosselin et al. (2013), this finding suggests that – despite many organisations introducing programmes to support family or caring needs – a disconnect exists between those policies and practices on the ground, arguably as a result of individuals' gendered 'world view'.

We discovered that the most significant disconnect between policy and practice on the ground which thus impacts on women's career advancement related to recruitment processes and power inequalities. Many participants described how their career pathways were obscured at times by being denied access to career development opportunities or due to blockages in recruitment processes (for example, a ranking system: a position in a hierarchy). This finding corresponds with Lee-Gosselin et al. (2013) who suggest that there is a lack of internal involvement that disconnects policy from practice. We also found that women professionals are not unaccepting of policy disconnects as many were taking advantage of organisational power in recruitment processes through accepting offers of promotion from their sponsors, i.e. without a formal recruitment process. Power inequality can also perpetuate the gender issue: '*I was singled out by the Chief Exec. to do a role that had been created for me. It wasn't necessarily right, but it certainly helped me*' [Professional 4].

The approach had positively impacted on her career advancement but also perpetuated the gender stereotype, in line with Morgan's (2006) metaphor of the 'psychic prison' in which social construction, attitudes and beliefs hold us back and constrain true change. Morgan (2006) unveils conscious and unconscious organisational processes and their enactment that shape the nature and culture of an organisation. People become limited by their ideas and belief systems leading to an incomplete and flawed understanding of reality. It is these socially constructed realities that take on an existence and power of their own and control those who created them. The influences that facilitate people and organisations to create the shared systems of meaning can become the constraints that prevent them from behaving in an alternative way.

There were many illustrations of both a positive effect and a negative effect on women's careers in the narratives. For some, this positive experience occurred from a strong relationship with mentors or sponsors, both men and women: '*my manager had definitely seen potential in me, she was always talking to me about potential, and eventually she shoe-horned a job for me*' [Professional 13]; '*she pushed me, the opportunities were there, if I wanted to take them*' [Professional 19]. For others, this power inequality had a negative impact:

> *I went for a role, it was a comparable role, and I thought that I should be okay. I knew one of those interviewing, and they know my strengths. I didn't get the job and found out they gave it to someone who worked in asset management, knows nothing about* [sector] *management, but he's the same age, from the same area as the two men who were 'appointing'. I can't help thinking there is still the old boy's network.*
> [Professional 17]

The narratives suggest that this 'sponsorship' approach can be more difficult in male-dominated cultures, where there can be intense and confrontational relationships with both men and women. The text below describes one participant's male colleague's reaction to her 'unexpected' promotion and confirmed her own personal feelings:

> *I did get quite a lot of flak, quite a lot of obstacles and challenge [...] they saw me as taking an opportunity away from them, 'well, you're going to get the job because you're a woman, and they need to tick the box' [...]. I was quite offended.*
>
> [Professional 14]

During the pre-workshop interviews, we asked the women if they had challenged any of the 'negative' recruitment decisions, and their response 'tests' the relevance and ability of so-called whistle-blowing-type policies that aim to provide assurance in recruitment processes. One of them reflects the views of others, illuminating the perception and inability to react:

> *It was fear of your position [...]. I thought I'm keeping out of this. I've got a job to do and a lot to do. I just need to get on and do it. It was widely known who would get the jobs before the interview, and it was generally male. You can't change any of this single-handedly.*
>
> [Professional 5]

Our analysis revealed that the women professionals did not lack aspiration or self-belief generally in pursuing their careers. However, one of the women stands out in some ways. She represents women who decide not to have children, in pursuit of their career. She made this decision in her twenties: '*I need to be 100 percent, and I couldn't be that, if there was a family. I wouldn't be able to cope*'. Throughout her career, Valerie had maintained 'tunnel vision' on her career path: '*I've always put one foot in front of the other*'. She recognised that this 'tunnel vision' may have obscured other opportunities but was determined and clear on where she wanted to be: '*I can take it to the next level of leadership, as opposed to just being the person who is led*' [Professional 18].

Further, two of the women had sought alternative lifestyles during their careers. For the first one, this review of her career and lifestyle had occurred regularly and involved occasionally working part-time and travelling for long periods: '*so whilst I may have had a career in local government that spanned 25 to 30 years [...] I had a defining moment every decade*' [Professional 4]. For the other, it was a step into entrepreneurship, aimed at providing flexibility of working hours, while caring for young children. A plan that had not come to fruition: '*I worked into the night and first thing in the morning [...] 6 days a week, so all the things I wanted to achieve, I didn't achieve'* [Professional 13].

Five women confirmed that they had reviewed their career aspirations between the ages of 50 and 60 and had critically appraised their organisational contexts and lifestyles. They had all felt a loss of other aspects of their identity and hoped for a future direction that would put more balance in their lives:

> *I was out of the house 12 hours a day if not longer, and would come home so tired [...]. When I stopped working* [for a while], *I baked a cake, I hadn't baked a cake for years and actually I quite enjoyed it [...], I enjoyed being a wife, [...] which I wasn't doing when I had been working. It was probably the first time I felt this is what a traditional, old fashioned wife situation is.*

[Professional 6]

For these women, the need to succeed in their careers had now been achieved, and their narratives show that they no longer feel driven or must prove their competence. They are now focussed on the things they want to do for themselves, with much variety from pursuing intellectual indulgence to relaxing in warmer climates.

2.3 So What Next?

In conclusion, and as anticipated, our findings were consistent with Senge's (1990) analogy of 'mental models' (generalisations and assumptions of how we view the world) (Senge, 2006) and Weick's (2006) equivalence of 'enactment' (re-enacted habits). We found that individuals were both consciously and unconsciously playing a role in creating and maintaining organisational cultures and were assisting in the recreation of patterns in gender relations. For example, they accepted promotion outside of formal recruitment processes, a finding that also corresponds with Cunliffe (2009a, p. 98) who highlights that:

> gender differences are created and maintained in organisational discourse and everyday interactions, a process of social construction in which both men and women produce and reproduce gender distinctions in conscious or unconscious ways by uncritically enabling and accepting those differences.

We agree with other researchers and writers that there has been an underachievement of the gender equality promise (van Eerdewijk and

Davids, 2014) and a lack of policy implementation for a variety of reasons: observations that gender is no longer of importance with resistance to change (Lombardo and Mergaert, 2013) to what is often seen as a 'tick box' exercise (de Vries, 2015); a lack of commitment to implement policies (Parpart, 2014); little attention paid to addressing fundamental structural causes and the need for cultural change, including stereotypes (van Eerdewijk and Davids, 2014); a focus on the technical agenda; and inadequate organisational resources to implement action and monitor effects (Parpart, 2014).

Gender mainstreaming faces important challenges, attains mostly symbolic results and does not fundamentally transform established policies or practices on the ground (Lee-Gosselin et al., 2013; Parpart, 2014). Essentially, resistance to change is based on the denial of systematic discrimination and gender stereotyping (Lee-Gosselin et al., 2013; Cunningham et al., 2014). Indeed, gender mainstreaming 'gets lost in the micro politics of practice' (van Eerdewijk and Davids, 2014, p. 396), is disappointing and can be labelled as a 'slow revolution' (Davids et al., 2014).

We found that the broader societal pressures to maintain the gendered *status quo* are very powerful and undermine efforts to transform gender relations and gendered structural inequalities ignoring the daily gender struggles that take place in all organisations. Despite a stock of analytical tools and gender experts, the transformative potential of gender equality remains questionable, with policy separated from practice, and where 'gender' has become a substitute for 'women', with a promise of inclusion rather than transformation coupled with non-binary and transgender which complicate the matter further.

Fundamentally, organisations have not tackled the underlying cultural issues that are 'sponsored' by social construction, and socially constructed realities are manifesting a power of their own. Simply, the 'blanket approach' taken by organisations is allowing gender stereotypes to perpetuate. This condition is influencing women's current status in the workplace and, at times, their ability to progress their careers.

In Chapter 3, we further the arguments made here by discussing gendered behaviours in organisations and the choices professional women make to further their careers.

3 Gendered Behaviour and Career Pathways

In Chapter 2 we argued that gender differences are created and maintained in everyday organisational transitions and that gender mainstreaming efforts in organisations have had little or no impact on women's career progression. We further those arguments in this chapter by discussing the extent to which gendered behaviours are evident in organisations and argue that professional women have made strategic choices to further their careers due to the failure of gender mainstreaming. These strategic choices not only impact the behaviours of the professional women themselves but also others in the workplace. To place the remainder of this chapter in the context of gender stereotypes, we begin with a brief discussion of gender as a social construct and of social role theory before moving on to consider professional women's early socialisation and life experiences and the impact of gender on their careers and leadership styles.

3.1 The Social Construct of Gender

As a social construct, gender can be described as being shaped and preserved by men and women, rather than a fixed quantity that one is born with. Childhood and adolescence are the peak times for the development of gendered behaviour, which is more or less passively acquired from the observation of social norms (Lippa, 2005). These early life and career development contexts can have an impact on career aspirations and career success in later life such as in relation to parental attitudes (Owen Blakemore and Hill, 2008) and can remain constant across a lifespan (Pallier, 2003). Every individual has a unique combination of social identities: for example, women, working career and the parental division of childcare. The terms 'masculine' and 'feminine' do not belong to either men or women, rather they are formed in the relationships between them and are emblematic. The social construction of gender emphasises the stereotypical norms dominant in Western culture that prescribe different roles to men and women and, in turn, strengthen the inequalities between them. As roles are carried forward to other contexts (for example, in leadership or in an employment setting), they contain gendered aspects of 'self' and 'others', assisting in the recreation of patterns in gender relations and power inequalities in society. These mental models are focussed on an awareness of the attitudes and perceptions that influence thought and interaction, encouraging individuals to assume certain characteristics, behaviours, roles and personalities.

Morgan's (2006) metaphor of the 'psychic prison' provides a way to consider how our social construction, attitudes and beliefs hold us back and constrain true change. Morgan (2006) discusses conscious and unconscious organisational processes and their enactment that shape the nature and culture of an organisation. People become limited by their ideas and belief systems leading to an incomplete and flawed understanding of reality. It is these socially constructed realities that acquire an existence and power of their own and control those who created them. The influences that facilitate people and organisations to create the shared systems of meaning can become the constraints that prevent them from behaving in an alternative way. The parallel between the organisation and those who work within it is the production and reproduction of organisational structures and processes that give dominance to traditional male values: for example, who is in power, who does what sort of work, what normative expectations influence behaviour and attitudes, what type of language is spoken and how individuals are rewarded and promoted (Cunliffe, 2009a).

The processes by which we shape and structure our realities are described by Weick (2006) as 'enactment', being the active role that we can unconsciously play in creating our organisations, our culture and our society. Weick (2006) also suggests that considering the 'enactment' of our socially constructed selves is shaping the current status of women in the workforce through those mental barriers. Indeed:

> gender differences are created and maintained in organisational discourse and everyday interactions, a process of social construction in which both men and women produce and reproduce gender distinctions in conscious or unconscious ways by uncritically enabling and accepting those differences.
>
> (Cunliffe, 2009a, p. 98)

In the UK today, many of our organisations have been typically built upon characteristics associated with Western male values. In light of those male values, many researchers agree that organisational context plays a crucial role in determining women's access to, and progression into, leader roles (Fitzsimmons and Callan, 2016; Hoyt and Murphy, 2016) or, indeed, their decisions to stay within that environment (Cheryan et al., 2009).

3.1.1 Social Role Theory

According to Eagly's (1987) social role theory, gender stereotypes develop from a division of labour that characterises society. Indeed: 'differences in the minds of men and women arise primarily from experience and socialisation' (Eagly and Wood, 1999, p. 414). It is the power of social roles and the environmental context to shape the behaviours of both men and women, which, in turn, determine people's stereotypes about men and women and are valid as they reflect real differences in the behaviours of men and women.

Constrained by gender roles to read to children and take care of the family, women show more nurturing behaviours, and, as a result, people perceive women to display 'communal' behaviours. Constrained by their roles to participate more in the competitive world of work, sports and public service, men display more assertive behaviours, and, as a result, people perceive men to display more 'agentic' behaviours (Heilman, 2012). The result of this lack of fit is that both men and women generally consider managerial roles as stereotypically more masculine than feminine and, therefore, professional women are perceived to be less qualified for leadership, although evidence suggests there is no substantial gender difference in leadership styles of behaviours (Seo et al., 2017). This is valid unless the organisational situation requires a leader of a more communal nature which may bring a different problem for women. The 'glass cliff' phenomenon (Ryan et al., 2016) holds that professional women gain promotion into more senior roles due to societal perceptions about the leadership attitudes they bring to the role; for example, a more nurturing style gives the perception that women are better equipped to handle difficult organisational situations. However, women's access to those high-level leadership positions in what are likely to be underperforming organisations is inherently risky and ultimately prone to failure.

Essentially, socially constructed views of ourselves are internalised and become unconscious working models that we bring to our gender and, in turn, our society and which accordingly silently permeates within organisational systems and leadership through gender stereotypes. Social construct theory and the metaphor of the psychic prison offer an explanation of why the characteristics of women and men that comprise gender stereotypes have been remarkably consistent over time, despite changes in society, economies and the world of work described earlier.

3.2 Influences of Gendered Roles

We found that all of the professional women who participated in our study had spent their childhood in gender stereotypical households, and that childhood influences were not a direct impact on their career however were certainly influential. Given the social construct of gender described above, this finding is not surprising because early childhood and adolescence are peak times for the development of gendered behaviours (Lippa, 2005), which can impact career aspirations and career successes in later life as each sex develops behavioural tendencies appropriate to observed gender roles (Owen et al., 2008). From the empirical data, we identified several key aspects of the influence of gendered roles in both 'at home' primarily parental influence and teachers' influence at school.

Christine's words are representative of all women with respect to the parental division of labour:

> *my mum would cook and clean and wash and iron, but my dad was very practical, so he'd do all the stuff around the house, maintain the car, so they both did their share, but in a very traditional way.*
>
> [Professional 14]

The women generally described their exposure to other aspects of life as gender stereotypical, both at home: '*when I told them I was playing rugby, my mam said why do you have to do a boys sport*' [Professional 14] and school: '*the boys got to carry the milk crates, whilst the girls got to give out the straws*' [Professional 13]. Many women felt that they had been more 'tom-boyish', rather than 'girly girls'. Joy's words are typical of others' sentiments: '*I've got skateboard scars [...]. I still wanted to look pretty. I always had long blond hair and pigtails*' [Professional 6].

Several women had parents whom they considered controlling or strict: '*my dad was quite domineering, so we were not allowed to wear make-up or nail varnish [...], we had to be in by a certain time, so it was quite a strict upbringing*' [Professional 1]. Some had support from elsewhere in the family, for example, older siblings: '*my older sister made me feel like I mattered* [Professional 1]. Several had strong mothers whom they felt had provided a good example to look up to: '*my mum always worked [...] she has been a role model [...] she is a very strong character*' [Professional 4].

Many women referred to being independent and resilient from an early age, which they felt had given them determination, and that is reflected in their stories. For a few, it felt 'forced' and out of financial necessity: '*I was pushed into work from 11 years old. I worked in the rock shop and made candy floss. I had to give half of my earnings over to the household*' [Professional 5]. For others, it was derived from the expectation of caring for themselves or their siblings from an early age: '*My brother and sisters were very much younger, I was always the babysitter full time*' [Professional 9]. All of the women had found this independence, and to some extent the resilience it generated, to be a valuable characteristic throughout their career journey.

3.2.1 Education and Career Influences

Many women felt that their educational endeavours were actively supported with university encouraged, and parents setting high expectations of them: '*my dad, a typical "forces" person, was quite strong willed, very authoritarian, and always pushed his kids to achieve a lot*' [Professional 6]. Whereas others had parents whom they felt were unsupportive and not interested: '*my mother didn't care if I went or not* [to school], *she never went to parents evening*' [Professional 17]; '*they viewed further education as something that wasn't necessary [...] you had to get into the workplace, [...] you didn't need education to do that for you*' [Professional 5]. For some, parents were just lacking in knowledge to provide career guidance: '*I don't think they've ever really understood what was out there or what was available to me. So whilst they've taken pride in my success, they've never felt pushy*' [Professional 4]; '*they probably didn't understand the importance of education, in a very serious sense*' [Professional 3]. For a few, this attitude was coupled with little encouragement at school, as in Daisy's reflection of her teacher's words: '*you will never make anything of yourself when you leave school*' [Professional 5]. At the very least, this was belittling for Daisy and she did prove her teacher wrong.

Five women demonstrated a determination to succeed in their career aspirations, recognising a need to return to education. At that time, four had caring responsibilities, and all continued to work full-time during this period. Daisy's story is representative of those women. In her narrative, she described the extent to which she had used multiple tactics to overcome a feeling that her 'education was not the best'. Her transcript had many examples of her approach, and her determination to acquire the skills and professional qualifications which she deemed necessary to be successful. Firstly, she recounts an early return to work from maternity leave:

> *I was on maternity leave when I was asked to consider going back to manage the office. I felt I had no choice because there may not be another opportunity. It was scary, because I didn't know if I had the skills and the ability to do it. I returned when my son was just 12 weeks old.*
>
> [Professional 5]

Secondly, reflecting on her journey to gain a degree:

> *I recognised that I needed a professional qualification to get anywhere in this sector. I couldn't go straight to the degree course, so I did a 'passport' onto a degree programme. I paid for myself to do this at college three nights a week* [whilst holding a full-time job]. *I then did day release to gain my degree.*
>
> [Professional 5]

We identified two prominent influences on women's careers. Firstly, we found that many professional women who had felt a lack of encouragement in their educational endeavours both by their parents and their school held on to a perceived lack of education. Consistent with the advice of prior authors (such as Kumra and Viddicombe, 2008) that career capital (increasing one's set of skills) is vital for career advancement, all the women in this situation had returned to education, gaining degrees or professional qualifications. Going further, the professional women described a high level of success in their careers, and a significant degree of self-confidence in their ability, despite their belief of 'educational inferiority' which had become 'life-long'. This perception, at times, had contributed to their feelings of self-doubt; for example, when working with individuals, they perceived to be more intelligent. This finding is consistent with Pallier (2003) who suggested that gender has a role to play in the level of self-assessment within the confidence paradigm, for example, learning the words you need to communicate and speaking those words with confidence.

It may also contribute to the mystery of why some women react to certain gender stereotype threats with ferocity and in a seemingly harsh manner. Accepting Steele's (1997) view that women are vulnerable to stereotype threat in terms of aspects that are perceived to be traditionally masculine, we would suggest that women in that culture, who face educational inferiority, can experience a 'collision' of gender stereotype threats, which can thus lead to an exacerbation of agentic behaviours.

Going further, we found that these women (with the exception of one) had experienced arousal of the gender stereotype threat in the arts-based workshop which was unexpected, as the teaching and learning environment was predominantly women, and arguably, the context of the arts and creativity was 'traditionally female'. This finding corresponds, to some extent, with the suggestion of Steele (1997, p. 614) that the threat is situational, effectively 'a threat in the air' because the threat had resulted from the women's belief that they were negatively stereotyped in their current activities. It may be that these women were encountering the threat of 'educational inferiority', as the arts-based activities connected intellect and emotion, and it was possible that the university setting for the workshops was an additional intimidation, thereby triggering a higher level of gender stereotype threat. The woman who felt educational inferiority, on the one hand, but did not feel a gender stereotype threat in the workshop, on the other hand, had a life-long career in 'the arts', and she considered herself 'to be very creative'.

This general lack of educational support in childhood and adolescence had also influenced early career decisions with many women having an unclear start to their careers, often becoming more career-focussed in their late twenties or early thirties. Many of these women had chosen career paths that were opportunistic, rather than planned, with their career choices linked to their personal beliefs, hobbies or their need for financial self-reliance. Only one participant had made the decision, in pursuit of her career, not to have children.

Consistent with the stereotype of a Northern woman – fortitude, grit and hardiness – the second prominent influence of childhood experiences on women's careers relates to the early development of strong characteristics associated with determination and resilience. We found that many women's narratives showed incredibly strong characteristics of fortitude, grit, spirit and hardiness, which we believe are the most successful characteristics in support of their career journeys. We found that all of the women placed a high value on a 'test' of leadership and made strives to offset any challenge or weakness they perceived through those strong characteristics in a 'where there's a will there's a way' type of attitude.

3.3 Gender Stereotypes in the Workplace

The formation of gender stereotypes can be described as both 'descriptive' and 'prescriptive' beliefs about people and their behaviours, that result in subtle and often invisible barriers for women that benefit men, while putting women at a disadvantage (Heilman, 2012). The basic consideration in descriptive gender stereotypes is the perceived 'lack of fit' between female stereotypes and leader stereotypes. This consideration is important in how people think about leaders. There has been considerable research in this area. Firstly, the 'think manager-think male' paradigm, which was noticed by Schein (1973) – being a comparison between leader stereotypes and male and female stereotypes. Secondly, the masculinity–femininity paradigm (traits or characteristics associated with being male or female, respectively) examined the nature of masculine versus feminine stereotypes of occupations (Shinar, 1975). Thirdly, complementing Schein's (1973) work, the agency–communion paradigm assessed the gender stereotypical essence of the leader stereotype (Powell, 1999). Despite the separate paradigms, all findings are relatively consistent across four decades with the masculine understanding of leadership and can be described as communal and agentic associations, being the beliefs people generally hold about men and women (Eagly and Karau, 2002).

On the other hand, prescriptive gender stereotypes establish normative expectations of the behaviour of men and women resulting in the devaluation and derogation of women, who directly or indirectly violate gender norms (Heilman, 2012). They dictate the norms of what attributes and behaviours are appropriate and inappropriate for men and women. For example, women should not demonstrate dominance, aggression, or achievement. It is well reported that violating these acceptable behaviours can create the 'backlash effect' from both a social and economic stance including hiring and promotion restrictions (Phelan et al., 2008), the display of interpersonal hostility (Heilman, 2012) and signs of being disliked by others (Heilman and Okimoto, 2007). In essence, being feminine while fulfilling agentic requirements is 'akin to walking a delicate tightrope' (Rudman and Glick, 2001, p. 759). Simply, societal effects cause women to be evaluated negatively if they are perceived as too feminine in their leadership style, as well as if they are perceived to be too masculine (Phelan et al., 2008). Therefore, the incompatibility between female gender roles and leadership roles remain a potent barrier to women's advancement to positions of leadership (Heilman, 2012). This incompatibility has had other pernicious effects on women's opportunities for leadership because it impacts women's behaviours and characteristics both in how they act towards others and in how they make individual decisions. For example, gender bias can occur as women in a position of power deal with female subordinates more critically than male subordinates, described as 'queen bee syndrome' (Derks et al., 2016), and 'double bind' being the contradictory forces for women of balancing agentic and communal behaviours (Varghese et al., 2018).

We now move on to illustrate the impact of gender stereotype threat and its implications for women's leadership styles. We then illustrate the strategic behaviours and choices made by the professional women to further their career by presenting several short vignettes.

3.3.1 Gender Stereotype Threat and Its Implications

The stereotype threat paradigm is the fear that a person's behaviour may confirm an existing stereotype of a group with which that person identifies (Steel, 1997). Any individual can be faced with the social–psychological threat of confirming or being reduced to a negative stereotype (Steele, 1997, 2010). Indeed, this threat may have a negative impact on 'intellectual functioning and identity development of individual group members' (Steele, 1997, p. 613). For example, men are vulnerable to stereotype threat in social contexts requiring emotional sensitivity (Davies et al., 2005), and women are vulnerable to stereotype threat in areas that are perceived as traditionally masculine (Steele et al., 2002). A further important point is that to experience stereotype threat someone does not need to believe the stereotype or even be worried that it is true of oneself (Steele, 1997, 2010). For example, a male manager in an office late at night with a woman colleague may fear that she may feel he may assault her, even though he does not believe the stereotype characterises him.

The detrimental impact of stereotype threat has been subject to intense study for many years and is well documented across a range of domains (von Hippel et al., 2011). For example, Kanter's (1977) seminal work, 'Men and Women of the Corporation', introduced a study of a large corporation, 'Indsco', in which the concept of 'tokenism' was introduced. In her study, Kanter suggests that, despite affirmative equality action efforts by the Corporation, the large majority of women remained concentrated in typically female jobs, and those who moved into management positions failed to achieve equality with men and women were 'often treated as representatives of their category, as symbols rather than individuals' (1977, p. 208). Kanter (1977) concluded that being the few among the many had a considerable impact, including women's treatment by others, but also women's behavioural responses to the differential treatment they receive which she suggested falls into three categories. Firstly, because of their obvious distinction to men, 'tokens' find an instant identity by conforming to pre-existing stereotypes becoming more visible and potentially offering themselves to be judged against the stereotypes. This phenomenon results in women working 'twice as hard' to have their achievements recognised. Secondly, 'tokens' are viewed as different from their male counterparts and may respond by either accepting outsider status or striving to become an insider, which interrupts, at times, the cultural life of the social masculine world. Finally, the 'dominants' tend to distort the characteristics and behaviours of the 'tokens' to fit their stereotypical image of the token category. Women can be thrust into the limelight and displayed as showpieces speaking for women, rather than themselves. Over 30 years later, this finding remains valid and corresponds with Cunningham et al. (2014), who suggested that outcomes from direct discrimination significantly impact three aspects: social capital – the networks of relationships among people who work in a particular society; self-efficacy – one's belief in one's ability to succeed; and chances for career progression.

Stereotype threat is considered to be generally contextual in that the threat arises whenever people become aware that they are negatively stereotyped in their current activities, described by Steele (1997, p. 614) as 'a situational threat – a threat in the air'. Common threats reported relate to negative performance and evaluative outcomes (Steele, 1997; Spencer et al., 1999), and other reported consequences more associated with 'feelings' (von Hippel et al., 2011). These factors include emotion (Brescoll, 2016), increased stress and anxiety (Shapiro and Neuberg, 2007) and disengagement or disidentification with the negatively stereotyped domain (Steele et al., 2002). Therefore, the threat can be seen to have wide-ranging effects on the individual beyond disrupting performance (von Hippel et al., 2011) including a lack of a self-confident demeanour (Amanatullah and Morris, 2010), negative behaviours of others (Heilman and Okimoto, 2007), lower leadership aspirations (Davies et al., 2005), self-directed bias through negative expectations of oneself (Haynes and Heilman, 2013) and self-defeating behavioural choices (von Hippel et al., 2011). Stereotypes can also have a negative impact on other aspects of organisational life, such as social and career capital (Eagly and Carli, 2007).

Career capital is described by Fitzsimmons and Callan (2016) as a set of skills an individual develops through his or her work and personal life, whereas social capital (Singh et al., 2006) refers to women's corporate networks and the reported benefits for women and their organisations.

According to Eagly and Carli (2007, p. 144):

> these informal ties are as essential to organisations as the human capital that allows competent work in the narrower, technical sense. Relationships build knowledge, trust, cooperation, and shared understanding.

An implication of gender stereotype threat is the professional women's ability to attain the required career and social capital in that: social representations show the persistent inequality in family responsibilities constraining women's involvement at work (McGowan et al., 2012); women have filtering points at different career stages, for example, child-bearing (Guillaume and Pochic, 2009); the perception that family responsibilities hinder women's commitment to an organisation (Walker et al., 2008); and expectations of long hours in the office create work–family conflict (Thebaud, 2015). Notwithstanding the view that research has oversimplified the interpretation of network differences by emphasising that women are denied access or have different preferences in the development of networks (Ibarra, 1993), the notion that men have more career and social capital than women is well reported (Fitzsimmons and Callan, 2016). Furthermore, a growing consensus has emerged among scholars that both are vital for women's career advancement (Kumra and Viddicombe, 2008) to ensure their visibility and, ultimately, to secure strong organisational sponsorship. Eagly and Carli (2007) agree and propose that women are aware of the need to build social capital to support their careers but are more thoughtful in how and when to develop networks by charting their way 'through the labyrinth'.

We found that in addition to the increasing career capital identified above, the majority of women recognised the need for and strive to develop social capital opportunities (social networking prospects) to support their career aspirations. Many of the women had gained sponsorship and had identified informal mentoring relationships and internal networks to support their ambitions. This finding is consistent with Eagly and Carli (2007), who propose that men may have more social capital than women, which is due to an array of other circumstances, rather than not understanding how organisations work. We found that women had different preferences than men in how and when they develop networks in that they carefully choose their allies and the timing of social networking, rather than take part in all social occasions on offer.

In summary, stereotype threat can depress a women's intellectual performance in the short run and, eventually, undermine identity itself, a predicament of serious consequence (Steele, 2010). Indeed, it has 'a great deal of potential to disrupt attitudes and behavioural intentions that many employers would regard to be of central importance' (von Hippel et al., 2011, p. 160). This aspect was demonstrated by Davies et al. (2005), whose participants were presented with gender stereotypical portrayals of women prior to being given a group task. The women (but not the men) were subsequently less interested in being the group leaders and were more interested in being followers (ibid). This activation of cultural stereotypes is inconsistent with the widely accepted views of leadership and thus can undermine leadership opportunity not only by eliciting doubts about stereotyped individuals' leadership abilities but also by making them personally anxious and confirming these doubts about taking on leadership roles (Eagly and Chin, 2010). It is important to note that not all women are impacted by all stereotype threats. For instance, research has shown that women who are confident about their leadership abilities are not deterred by statements that women have less leadership ability than men but instead react by exhibiting even more competence (Hoyt and Blascovich, 2010).

3.4 Gender Stereotypes, Leadership Style and Career Advancement

Gender stereotypes are evident in all of the women's narratives, thereby impacting their potential for career progression. The most common themes are reflected and many readers will recognise themselves in the text. We will initially focus on two areas: firstly, 'balancing agentic and communal attributes' which discusses the extent to which women adapt their leadership style and put effort into their public image to make them acceptable in their 'masculine' organisational worlds. Secondly, 'setting high performance standards and performance evaluation' which discusses the extent to which women expect high standards of themselves and self-evaluate against those standards. We then move onto discuss the impact of early career influences and organisational culture.

3.4.1 Balancing Agentic and Communal Attributes

All narratives confirm that women embrace agentic attributes, together with communal attributes, which create a sense of disorder: '*sometimes I have to be authoritarian, and sometimes I can be completely myself and anything in between, the best way to describe it is, it's a mess*' [Professional 14].

For many women, the choice was how to balance different frames of behavioural judgement within cultural norms. This choice was particularly evident for women in male-dominated cultures and for those involved in organisational change. Thirteen narratives fit within the latter, resulting in additional pressures that were central to an increase in agentic behaviours. Kayley's narrative in Vignette 1 is representative, with more detail in Appendix 1 (Case Study 4).

Vignette 1   Balancing Agentic and Communal Attributes

Kayley is a senior human resources executive, and her text demonstrates the co-existence of agentic and communal attributes. In her transcript, she confirms what portrays effective leadership to her and was clear in her description: 'resilience, self-confidence, action orientated, honest, open and transparent'. Kayley's text presents her as a people person, a team player: 'even if I'm in the thick of an issue, I am humane'. She describes making a deliberate shift away from adopting her typically feminine approach, towards the adoption of a male subject position, when a gender stereotype threat was aroused: 'I need to be dominant, when taking on a man in the workplace. I don't want to walk into a room, and let a man think that he is messing on me'. Her transcripts contain many examples of ways in which she learned to think like a man in some aspects of her work: 'He does budgets and I do people. We clash like hell when we are in a group setting. It's about me being dominant. I'm ready for a fight, I'm ready to take him on. My worst characteristics are brought out when I'm in male company'.

[Professional 13]

Without exception, the women's narratives expressed an expectation that they should embrace a more feminine and distributive approach to leadership, and yet this expectation combines with tension: '*I am passionate and caring, but not tactile. I display empathy and female characteristics, but I can be hard if I need to be*' [Professional 17]; '*I can be incredibly sympathetic if somebody is in tears, but it wears thin if it's around performance*' [Professional 5]; '*I do get argumentative. I don't shy away from conflict [...] I'm not confrontational, but I will stand my ground*' [Professional 3]. Many texts also make reference to the desire to show affiliative tendencies of promoting harmony and collaboration: '*it's give and take, rather than I'm the boss*' [Professional 7]; '*I want the team to work for me because they want to, not because I'm the boss and I've told them to*' [Professional 6].

The women's stories demonstrate that this tension is enhanced by a greater predominance of agentic behaviours. For many, these behaviours were displayed as autonomy, self-reliance and decisiveness: '*I was always good at what I did. I always worked really really hard, and did over and above*' [Professional 17]. For others, it exhibited as action orientated or achievement focussed: '*when you're managing a project and it's all going "belly up", [...], I go into "Attila the Hun" mode*' [Professional 6]. For some, it was the inclination to take charge: '*I don't take any crap from them* [men], *I'll be quite hard and I come away feeling like I've kicked a puppy*' [Professional 5].

For many women, this increase in agentic behaviours incorporates introducing new language which seemed natural to them: '*someone had just given me a piece of work [...] I said well that looks s***, it just came out of my mouth*' [Professional 19]. This revised communication style was particularly evident in one participant's communication with men: '*if I give you this chance and you make a t*** of me [...], it was that kind of conversation that upon reflection is very male*' [Professional 4]. For some, there was a distinction between the language appropriate for men, rather than women: '*I have found myself acting more masculine [...], you start maybe throwing in a few swear words [...]. I can't ever imagine having to act or talk like that if it had been a female employee*' [Professional 4].

For a few women, displaying agentic behaviours was problematic, because it affected how others responded to them and revealed subsequent emotions:

> *I realised that she wasn't ready for the challenge [...]. She just threw a load of stuff at me, deflection, she was angry. I don't feel sad very often, but it made me feel sad that I'd had that impact on her [...]. I felt like I'd crushed her and that's not nice.*
>
> [Professional 13]

For a few, it was confusing to be on the receiving end of such behaviours and could lead to significant decisions. Joy's narrative in Vignette 2 is representative.

Vignette 2 Deciding to Leave

Joy describes how she had felt hurt and deceived when her new female Chief Executive, who she saw as an ally, withdrew her support. Joy, working with her experience and skill, tried to balance the agentic behaviours displayed by her new CEO, with her own leadership style of openness and honesty. It was apparent that the more communal approach was unimportant to the new CEO, and this brought Joy into conflict with her: '*I got to the point where I didn't know if I was coming or going*'. Joy speaks forcefully of the need for interpersonal dynamics to be appreciated as important aspects of organisational life. She had spoken out for staff and their values, but the CEO had other priorities. Despite her seniority and expertise, Joy did not feel she was being ascribed the influence she warranted and resigned her position.

[Professional 6]

Consistently in the women's narratives, male-dominated environments provided the setting where strained relationships with other women occurred most frequently, with interpersonal hostility and signs of being disliked by others commonplace. These experiences were making women's lives demanding and had a significant impact on behaviours and feelings. Linda's narrative in Vignette 3 is representative, with more detail in Appendix 1 (Case Study 3).

Vignette 3 Interpersonal Hostility and Self-doubt

Linda presents herself as confident, ambitious and resilient. In her pre-workshop transcript, Linda described a 'blockage' to her career progression, instigated by her line manager, with whom she had a difficult relationship. She believed her line manager was obeying 'instruction' from a senior male officer, which was typical in her male-dominated environment. This had left Linda feeling angry, confused and frustrated: '*I was disappointed at her for not standing up for me as a woman, [...] or one of her direct reports*'. Linda felt undervalued, and demoralised, and this experience had led to her feeling self-doubt.

[Professional 14]

3.4.2 Setting High Standards

In keeping with agentic behaviours, the transcripts confirmed without exception that women set high standards for themselves, which they believed were necessary to progress their careers: '*If you put in over and above, give something your all, you'll be rewarded. I've always found that to be the case*' [Professional 4], or connected to a concern for organisational effectiveness: '*I was working myself into the ground; everything I produce had to be spot on*' [Professional 8].

Most of the women believed that they were doing their jobs well in those terms, but working to this high standard often proved difficult. For many, it would mean working very long hours: '*if I had to be there 14 hours a day, I would be there 14 hours a day*' [Professional 5], and it provided a frame of reference against which performance could be evaluated by oneself and others. The vast majority of women talked about the importance of knowing they were performing well against their self-imposed targets and in the eyes of others. This aspect was important to their self-image: '*I have a bar, and then I have a bar above it, and people expect that. Then I expect that of me, and if I fall short of that, even if I've met that bar, I am irritated at me*' [Professional 18]. For some, it was just signifying that they had a boss who was difficult. Daisy's story is representative of others:

> *She would ask you for things and then mark them in a red pen, because it wasn't done in her style. It wasn't necessarily wrong [...]. I got to a point where I thought there is nothing you can do here that's going to be right.*
>
> [Professional 5]

This lack of positive feedback can be highly detrimental to individuals, and becomes self-reinforcing, as in Daisy's case: '*she makes me feel I wasn't clever enough to do the job, she belittled me*' [Professional 5]. Daisy was unable to obtain evaluations of her performance and started to doubt her own competence: '*I thought I couldn't get a job anywhere else, because I can't write a report*' [Professional 5]. Daisy had kept her self-doubt to herself, reducing opportunities for receiving contradictory, more positive feedback. Only later did she discover that other colleagues also had difficulties with this individual: '*after she left there was all kinds of stuff that came out about her, and [...] people saying thank goodness she's gone*' [Professional 5]. She was then able to increase her self-evaluation.

For others, de-valuing feedback confirmed the culture of the organisation, as in Kaitlen's narrative as she was reminded of her place in her male-dominated environment: *'you are the probationer, you are the lowest of the low, you never ask a rank to do anything [...] don't you ever do that again'* [Professional 13].

Jordan had a similar experience but had found a way to legitimise the self-doubt she was feeling by reducing the effort she put into the task:

> *you produce an annual report, and people always pull it apart. It doesn't matter how good it is [...] it doesn't matter if it's right or wrong, [...] it makes you feel bad, whereas* [with less effort], *you can think, well yes, okay, I didn't spend long on it.*
>
> [Professional 8]

We found that, without exception, women had adapted their leadership style, embracing both agentic and communal behaviours, believing that this adaptation would make them more 'acceptable' in the 'masculine worlds'. This finding corresponds with the early paradigms of gender theorists (Schein, 1973; Shinar, 1975; Powell, 1999) who all suggest a masculine understanding of leadership. We also found that this phenomenon frequently led to negative consequences from two perspectives. Firstly, women presenting highly agentic behaviours often faced interpersonal hostility from other women (for example, being challenged in their decision-making). This finding corresponds with various authors (Eagly and Carli, 2007). Secondly, women with strong communal behaviours often felt signs of being disliked by other women and were ostracised or 'cold-shouldered'. This finding is consistent with Phelan et al. (2008), who argues that women can be evaluated negatively if they are perceived as too feminine in their leadership style, as well as if they are perceived to be too masculine. This finding also corresponds with Phelan and Rudman's (2010) notion that violating acceptable behaviours can create the 'backlash effect' (reprisals from behaving counter-stereotypically), and many women agreed that this process is 'akin to walking a delicate tightrope' (Rudman and Glick, 2001, p. 759). We suggest, therefore, that this type of behaviour is extensive. This finding parallels Heilman (2012), who suggests that the violation of descriptive gender stereotypes (perceived 'lack of fit' between female stereotypes and leader stereotypes) and prescriptive gender stereotypes (normative expectations for the behaviour of men and women) are likely to result in stereotype-based bias.

Going further, we found that many women were content with being viewed through two lenses of agentic and communal styles of leadership, and that they consider their leadership as 'firm, but fair' despite, at times, this perception leading to tense relationships with others. This finding is characteristic of Bass et al.'s seminal work (1996) describing a 'transformational' style of leadership, and Eagly and Johannsen-Schmidt's (2001) suggestion that individuals focus on the development and mentoring of their followers. Extending this concept, we found that agentic and communal attributes can co-exist seamlessly, with women displaying a remarkable ability to swiftly adapt and modify behavioural attributes in response to organisational situations (for example, when giving negative performance feedback to a female subordinate who displayed negative emotion, then communal behaviours increased).

As previously suggested, within the realm of agentic attributes, we found that many women set self-determined high standards which they believed were necessary to progress their careers, protect their self-image and prove their effectiveness within their organisations. We found that this demonstration of professionalism and effectiveness was a particularly important strategy for women when dealing with a situation that was not an everyday event (for example, in dealing with a disciplinary hearing of a male subordinate).

Going further, we found that, in setting high standards for themselves and striving for 'perfection', these women increase the likelihood of experiencing gender stereotype threat as they self-evaluate their own performance against those self-imposed standards. We found that this situation reinforced self-doubt, which resulted in negative feelings towards those providing the negative evaluation, which could be long-lasting. This finding corresponds with the seminal work of Steele and Aronson (1995) who claim that being evaluated through the lens of negative stereotypes can focus a person's attention on the negative aspects of a stereotype, which can serve to undermine anticipated outcomes. We also found that feelings of self-doubt could lead to self-defeating behavioural choices, for example, seeking alternative employment.

Therefore, we found that by exercising their influence and power, women can feel considerable negative emotion, and concealing this negative emotion is a vital strategy in their day-to-day working lives. This perception reflects a reality to a certain extent. However, it nonetheless does have a variety of negative consequences for women in their career potential if emotional self-control is not maintained; for example, it can result in negative performance feedback and thereby can hinder career advancement. This finding is characteristic of Shield's (2002, p. 11) 'emotional master stereotype', where showing emotion heightens the prevalence and relative magnitude of the gender stereotype threat because 'it serves as an overarching organising principle for other related beliefs' (ibid). Consistent with Brescoll (2016), who suggests that the impact of chronically trying to navigate emotional double-binds at work is significant, we found that controlling emotion creates a considerable tension for women as they attempt to balance frames of behavioural judgement in their organisational settings, i.e. when should emotion be shown, as well as not be shown. We are reminded of Shapiro and Neuberg's (2007, p. 111) claim that 'academic performance may be neither the most important consequence of stereotype threat nor the most effective measure for inferring its existence'. Hilary Clinton described the dilemma:

> *you have to be aware of how people will judge you for being, quote, 'emotional'. As so it's a really delicate balancing act … how you navigate what is still a relatively narrow path – to be yourself, to express yourself, to let your feelings show, but not in a way that triggers all of the negative stereotypes.*

(Clinton, 2010)

We found that the effects of concealing negative emotion caused stress and anxiety that led (at times) to decreased job satisfaction and commitment and increased the likelihood of work withdrawal.

3.4.3 Early Career Influences

What is interesting in the narratives is that 13 of the professional women had vague starts to their careers. Eight of the women started in lower-level jobs and then consciously became more career orientated in their late twenties or early thirties. Four of the women had children and/or were married and then later re-returned to employment. Two of the women were 'introduced' to their career by a friend. For others, a strong sense of self-confidence was apparent in their early career, as was finding a job. This self-confidence had allowed them to meet their passion and begin to demonstrate their capabilities in their early twenties. Seven women's narratives revealed career choices that connected to their personal beliefs developed at an early age: '*it fits my personality, my politics, my everything about me. Fighting for people's rights. Yes, that's what I can do*' [Professional 7], or hobbies that became career choices: '*my career to date has been in an area of work that is also what I'm passionate about, and is also my hobby*' [Professional 18]. For nine of the women, financial self-reliance was a significant aspect of their career decisions, and for a few, this was a difficult decision: '*I wanted to be with my kids [...] I really didn't want to leave the boys, but for financial reasons I had to go to work*' [Professional 1].

Many professional women had identified role models or sponsors at various times throughout their careers, to support career advancement. For many, it was recognition and being singled out through working hard, while demonstrating ambition: '*I always wanted to do things, work hard, and get on [...] I ended up being promoted again quite quickly*' [Professional 3]. For a few, it was gaining sponsorship and financial support to return to education: '*I would really like to do a PhD, but I can't afford it [...] she said [sponsor], go and ask the chief officer [...] so I got the PhD*' [Professional 2]. For others, particularly at the beginning of their career, it was identifying role models who displayed behaviours and attributes that 'fit' with their beliefs, to allow for personal growth and aspiration: '*she was really resilient, dead strong, like power to the people type of person that I love, really positive*' [Professional 11].

3.4.4 Organisational Culture

All of the professional women's narratives describe organisational cultures as having an impact on their working lives. The most prominent dissatisfaction came from 15 participants who were working in what they termed as 'male-dominated cultures'. This included male-dominated environments where less than 10% of employees in the organisation(s) were women and patriarchal organisations where males were considered to hold primary power at the top of the organisation.

All of the women's narratives display a prominent feature of male-dominated organisational cultures across all sectors as having an impact on their career development. This culture, where typically male values are reinforced, often represented an organisational environment that was harsh and tough. The narratives confirmed this finding in both working relationships with men and with women.

Many narratives contained reference to managers dealing with each other in a blunt and direct manner. For Daisy, this direct and assertive language with men had developed over many years of working in male-dominated organisational cultures. She confirmed that she viewed her male colleagues as 'low performers': '*I see male counterparts as being quite ineffective and quite inefficient*' [Professional 5]. She described how she had spoken to a male subordinate who she assessed as underperforming: '*you need to grow a pair [...] and go out there and deal with it*' [Professional 5]. For Linda, the bluntness in her language was directed at her female line manager who she felt had 'blocked' her access to a leadership development programme: *'where the hell are your f****** values'* [Professional 14]. The narratives also confirmed that this direct manner could present as a 'backhanded compliment'. Joy's narrative described a male colleague's 'compliment' following her success at dealing with a difficult and highly political issue in her organisation: *'you have the biggest set of cojones on a woman I've seen'* (*a Spanish word sometimes used as a euphemism for testicles*) [Professional 6].

For others, expectations for career progression were made clear. Linda and Kaitlen's narratives are representative as they described advice from male colleagues: *'you have to be seen to stand toe to toe with a man, and win that "shouty" argument, so they don't see you as a little girl'* [Professional 14]; *'you need to affiliate yourself to somebody, almost like a sponsor, somebody who is high up [...] and they will help you progress'* [Professional 12]. In this environment, the women's narratives contained many individual ways of coping with cultural pressures, thereby creating acceptable identities. For many, it was downplaying gender to meet the perceived positive image of themselves. Veronica's text is representative. She was in the early stages of her career. Her narrative presents her as confident, ambitious and seeking opportunities to make a positive impression: *'I'm a quick learner, so if you show me something I'll get stuck in'* [Professional 19]. Her narrative describes how she prepares to chair a meeting in her male-dominated environment: *'if you can imagine walking into a room of 15 males, all quite burly, [...] I turn off the girly, and turn on the "right", I'm in a meeting. I just switch off to it'* [Professional 19]. For a few, downplaying gender had become the 'norm' and was becoming difficult. Samantha's narrative in Vignette 4 reflects her difficult career journey and feelings towards the image she feels compelled to present, with more detail in Appendix 1 (Case Study 2).

Vignette 4 Downplaying Gender

Samantha had been the first woman in the position of export manager. Her first months in her organisation were confusing and shocking, as she realised that all of the women were in administrative roles, and she was the only woman in management. Samantha soon learned that her professional expertise was not welcomed in the organisation: *'they didn't support me'*, *'they feared me'*. During her time in this role, Samantha felt she had no choice but to focus on her work. She felt extremely lonely and isolated, as she tried to balance her behaviours in this challenging environment: '*I'm like a contradiction, I'm hard and I'm soft both at the same time*'. '*I want to feel wholesome, and no longer lonesome*'.

[Professional 16]

For some, it was becoming one of the boys to 'fit' in their organisation: '*I can't tell you how many women I've heard say, I just want to fit in with the lads*' [Professional 14]. Many narratives describe developing relationships with men as a working strategy: '*I can be as "blokey" as most of them, if I need to be*' [Professional 5]. For others, this strategy had resulted from difficult relationships with women: '*I tend to be more friendly with men than women, but that's because of my past experience [...] of being backstabbed by women*' [Professional 1]. For a few, becoming one of the boys did not 'fit' with their gendered beliefs and appeared to interrupt 'normal life' for men in male-dominated environments: '*they drink on the train, they drink in the pubs, there has been discussion of a strip club in the past. That's not something I would do*' [Professional 14].

All narratives confirmed extensive and daily gender stereotypic attitudes and behaviours across all sectors, displayed by both men and women. The attitudes and behaviours can be subtle: '*he doesn't stand and scream and shout, it's more that type of subtle behaviour. Constantly giving people very tight deadlines to do things [...], and then he's disappointed*' [Professional 14], and unsubtle, experienced by Daisy in comments from a male colleague following her promotion: '*oh great; she'll be pregnant before we know it, so she will not be around for very long*' [Professional 5].

Many texts included reference to discriminatory language aimed directly at individual women, for example, in relation to dress: '*he said to me: "just wear a short skirt and show a bit of cleavage"*' [Professional 5]. The data also confirmed many instances of the cultural acceptance of the language used, in certain circumstances, perpetuating the gender stereotype, as illustrated in Julie's words:

all the 'titty' posters would be turned around really quickly because they would get sacked for it [...] they were guys over a certain age, who have been plumbers for 40 years and sometimes you do cut them a bit of slack.

[Professional 10]

This harsh and tough environment can lead to feelings of dissatisfaction with individuals starting to question their current environments and seeking alternative professions, as in Linda's narrative in Vignette 5, with more detail in Appendix 1 (Case Study 3).

Vignette 5 Starting to Question Working in a Male-dominated Environment

An array of factors began to contribute to the questioning that eventually led Linda to consider seeking a new role outside of her male-dominated environment. The questioning was partly prompted by the blockages in promotion opportunities: '*I'm just going to go somewhere new where I can see there's a career path*'. She was also feeling the cost of acting 'out of character': '*I'm not averse to making my presence felt, but I'm disappointed if I have to get to that stage*'. Later, Linda emphasised her continuing faith in the kind of culture her organisation was striving to develop: '*I've gone through the whole change curve of fury, to upset, to anger, to I'm just going to get another job to no, I'm going to fight this, and I'm going to be the one that breaks through for other people*'. For the time being, Linda remains in her role.

[Professional 14]

We found that the atmosphere in male-dominated environments seems to be harsher and tougher than other environments, with a rawness that seemed surprisingly outdated. This apparently hostile working environment had higher levels of discrimination depicted by both men and women. Going further, professional women who were outside of a male-dominated environment became aware of the seismic scale that gender stereotype threat played for some. The stories made significant impressions on the professional women and ourselves as researchers, as we observed the visible impact upon those women sharing their stories. It was evident that women in male-dominated environments experience more barriers and greater stress in their pursuit of a career than those in other environments. Disappointingly, this finding is consistent with Steele et al.'s (2002, p. 385) commentary that there is a 'concrete, real-time threat of being judged and treated poorly in settings, where a negative stereotype about one's group applies' and continues to be relevant in more recent research. For example, Cunningham et al. (2014) confirm that there is interpersonal mistreatment and marginalisation of women when they are part of a less powerful group. We also found that this environment can undermine a woman's sense of belonging in the chosen field, and her motivation and desire to pursue success, resulting in seeking employment 'where there is a clear career path'. This finding corresponds with Cheryan et al. (2009).

We found that the pattern of interaction in male-dominated environments seemed very similar to the classic dynamics of tokenism suggested by Kanter (1977) where 'tokens' or minority status leads to more stereotypic characterisations. Further, we found that organisational cultures, permeating a competitive ethos, were more threatening, especially as women moved further up the hierarchy into leadership roles. At times, this mobility increased the level of gender stereotype threat, resulting in women feeling a need to 'hold their own', which they displayed by increased agentic behaviours.

We also found that organisational context played a different role on the career aspirations of women over the age of 50. These women had all appraised their lifestyles, resulting in (to some extent) reduced 'career drive' and an increased need to 'do something for themselves'. We found a sense that they were seeking a new identity, resulting from a tiredness of maintaining an imitation of themselves (the public image), although this effort became less important as they approached another stage in their careers. There was also an acceptance that 'it's too late for me' to change gender stereotypical cultures. We realised that these women had experienced a depletion of their organisational life energy, and regaining a sense of balance in their lives was of considerable importance to them.

3.5 Impact on Career Pathways

As anticipated, our findings were consistent with Senge's (1990) analogy of 'mental models' (generalisations and assumptions of how we view the world) (Senge, 2006), and Weick's (2006) equivalence of 'enactment' (re-enacted habits). We found that individuals were both consciously and unconsciously playing a role in creating and maintaining organisational cultures and were assisting in the recreation of patterns in gender relations, for example, by downplaying being a woman or in decision-making influenced by the social construct of gender.

Many women had a vague start in their careers typically driven by a gender stereotypical upbringing, combined with the challenges of their socially constructed organisational realities. Despite these antecedents, the professional women had been relatively successful in their careers to date in that they had encapsulated the 'test' of leadership and had a resolve to succeed. A contributing factor to their success may be the display of North East women's stereotypical behaviours of independence, resilience and a sheer determination to succeed alongside strong characteristics of fortitude, grit, spirit and hardiness, which we believe are the most successful characteristics in support of their career journeys. All of the professional women had made efforts to offset any challenge or weakness they perceived through those strong characteristics in a 'where there's a will, there's a way' type of attitude.

In their determination to succeed, the women had also made a wide range of timely and strategic choices to support their career aspirations in that: many women had increased their career capital by returning to education at various stages of their career development, all had carefully chosen internal networks to fit their present career requirements and many had 'hand-picked' mentoring relationships or organisational sponsorship. Some of this activity had involved women in downplaying their gender to create a positive image of their 'leader selves' or to enhance the relationships within their masculine powerbase. All of these factors had supported the perpetuation of gender stereotypes and augmented power inequalities.

We also found that in addition to the increasing career capital identified above, the majority of the professional women recognised the need to develop social capital opportunities (social networking prospects) to support their career aspirations. Many of the women had gained sponsorship and had identified informal mentoring relationships and internal networks to support their ambitions. We found that women had different preferences from men in how and when they develop networks in that they carefully choose their allies and the timing of social networking, rather than participating in all social occasions on offer.

The impact of the social construct of gender had a greater emphasis for women working in male-dominated environments and those environments with a competitive ethos. In those male-cultured environments, women faced greater levels of harshness and discrimination compared to those in mixed or female-dominated environments, and similar to the classic dynamics of 'Tokenism' suggested by Kanter (1977), they were more likely to face barriers to their career progression, and were also more likely to perceive a sense of 'not-belonging'. These experiences, in turn, caused the women to exhibit higher levels of stress and anxiety. Disappointingly, there has been little progress since 2002 when Steele et al. (2002) highlighted that women experience more barriers and greater stress in their pursuit of a career in a male-dominated environment. There was also a higher occurrence of women in this environment seeking alternative employment to mediate the perceived gender stereotype threat.

All the professional women had adapted their leadership style and public image to one they perceived to be more acceptable in their masculine organisational worlds. Within this revised leadership style, women had invariably set themselves high performance standards against which they self-assessed, and – as fundamentally – they gave others 'permission' to do the same. Any negative performance assessment consistently led to perceived gender stereotype threat and increased self-doubt. Further exploration identified that this change in leadership style had increased the likelihood of women to violate 'gender norms', as they attempted to balance descriptive gender stereotypes (women's fit with leadership), alongside prescriptive gender stereotypes (normal expectations of behaviours for women – or norms). Any violation of gender norms regularly had a negative impact from both or either a social and economic perspective (for example, interpersonal hostility or blockages in career development opportunities). Many of the professional women had a negative reaction to a violation of gender norms; they also demonstrated a remarkable ability to swiftly adapt their behavioural attributes to a more 'transformational' style of leadership to counteract the perceived violation.

Further, we found that professional women show a higher level of agentic behaviours or increased self-doubt in the specific context where two (or more) gender stereotype threats were activated. For example, a 'collision' of 'educational inferiority' (stemming from a lack of encouragement in childhood), and a learning environment that was creatively challenging (traditionally feminine), or in an 'educational' setting, all of which heightened the perceived gender stereotype threat.

The women displayed a considerable level of tension resulting from their desire to conceal the 'emotional master stereotype' of heightened negative emotion. A contributing factor to this increased tension may be that as women perceive the gender stereotype threat (the negative evaluation by others), their emotional anxiety is increased – thereby creating a self-fulfilling prophecy.

Interestingly, we found that women in the third (or higher) phase of their careers had reduced career drives and a sense of 'burn-out' in maintaining imitations of themselves (the public image). Contributing factors may have been the additional 'competitive ethos' of their organisational change agendas and the opportunity to transition to the next career stage. Chapter 4 focusses on the workshop design and insights from the workshops and post-workshop interviews, where we indicate how deep reflection and making sense of the gendered behaviours in the workplace affected the women participants.

4 Workshops and Their Outcomes

4.1 Workshop Design

We wanted to explore arts-based methods that were quite different to typical diversity interventions. Inspiration for the workshops came partly through the literature review, in particular Olivier and Verity's (2008) paper 'Rehearsing tomorrow's leaders: the potential of "mythodrama"'; and attendance at the Art of Management Organisation conference 2016 in Bled, Slovenia. At the conference, one of the authors was introduced to a consultant and researcher of CoCreation based in Copenhagen, Denmark, who in 2010 had successfully completed his doctoral work on arts-based methods in management education at Cranfield School of Management.

In Workshop One – 'Sense-making', the exercises allowed participants to experiment through the use of new and unfamiliar styles, ideas and behaviours, for example, free style writing, photography. It was very much an 'in the moment' experience, with participants exploring what they were feeling in the 'here and now'. In Workshop Two, 'Mythodrama', the exercises were a more traditional approach, for example, group work with flip charts and post-it notes, with participants exploring how they might react in similar circumstances: fundamentally, a more future-focussed learning style. We present the two workshop designs in the following sections.

4.1.1 Workshop One – 'Sense-making'

Workshop One – 'Sense-making' focussed solely on sensory experiences which 'demanded' that participants look deeply into themselves (Table 4.1). The workshop applied primarily an individualistic approach, and was subject matter centred, with each participant focussed on their own individual and current problem. This prompted a high level

Table 4.1 Structure of Workshop One: 'Sense-making'

Approximate timing (min)	Activity	Description
20	Introductions and setting the scene	Facilitator-led conversation focussed on introducing the facilitator, participants and specific work context.
25	Identification of a core problem in the workplace	Focus on the dominating culture in the workplace; selecting concrete difficult situations and making sense of them.
15	Guided relaxation	Facilitator-guided relaxation focussing on the senses (body scanning).
100	Metaphorical engagement	Describing experience (problem) in sensory words and photographic expressions.
60	Lunch break	Informal conversations between participants, facilitator and researcher.
60	Confidence exercise, metaphorical engagement and active listening	Expressing the sense of 'settledness'. A reflective discussion on positive experiences of your 'settledness' and how one can achieve confidence. A reframing, positive psychology approach.
20	Meditation	Facilitator-guided meditation focussing on the awareness of being a mountain as a metaphor for confidence.
45	Relaxation	Body scanning and invitation to release the tension.
20	Wrap up	Reflection on the day and closing.

of engagement with the subject. It was also constructivist in nature, allowing participants to construct their own knowledge related to the issue of focus.

Workshop One was facilitated by Dr Claus Springborg specialising in leadership development. His main focus is the development of self-knowledge through arts-based methods, contemplative practices and meditation. His work is grounded in neuroscience and rich personal experience. In his work with managers, he blends his research findings with his experience as a dancer, musician and mediation teacher.

This session started with **Introductions**, which were mostly facilitator-led. The conversation focussed on introducing the facilitator, all of the participants and the nature of sensory experiences. The introduction stressed the importance of the specific work context and industry or organisational culture.

The first session dedicated to the **Identification of a core problem in the workplace.** Participants focussed on the dominant culture in their workplace and how they fit with that culture (or not). Throughout the activity, the facilitator encouraged thoughts around 'feelings': How does it feel to have a particular issue to deal with? How does our body react? How do we adjust to cope? Talking about the 'concrete' experience helped ground feelings and reaction in a work context, initiating sense-making of difficult situations and the realisation of commonalities while building rapport between participants. We noted that this exercise pushed some participants outside of their comfort zone.

Following this session, the facilitator introduced a guided relaxation exercise, focussing on the senses through the **body scanning** exercise. In this session, the participants were asked to bring their thoughts to the present and notice body sensations in their legs, stomach and breathing. It was a grounded, calming and focussed activity.

The next session involved **Metaphorical engagement**. First the participants engaged in non-stop writing for 10 minutes focussed on describing their core problem in **sensory words**. They then created a poem describing how they were feeling when faced with their core problem (examples: 'frustration', 'dark', 'hot', 'anxious', 'fast'). They were asked to make use of the sensory words they had listed in the first part of this exercise. There is further discussion on sense-making and metaphor in Chapter 5 in Sections 5.4 and 5.5.

Following this session, they took a number of photographs that would trigger the same sensory feeling. Each participant was asked to read their poem and say a few words about their images **(photo expressions)**. Noticing the change of how women talk about the situations, not as an abstract 'objective' situation, but how it felt, what it meant to them as individuals. At the end of the activity, there was no reflection or conclusions drawn out in relation to participants' problems: rather the focus was on what was immediately interesting.

The following session explored the positive experience of **'settledness'** in participants' lives. In groups of three, they had five minutes to talk about how we can achieve confidence. The group feedback emphasised the importance of validating, acknowledging, listening without judgement and positive regard. The facilitator explained that we often think that confidence is 'dependent' on various factors that are usually external to us ('I will feel confident if/when ...'). **Confidence** is something that is with us ALL of the time (reframing). We need to stop putting conditions on positive feelings. It is about striving for 'settledness' rather than reactionism.

This exercise was concluded by facilitator-guided **meditation** focussing on the awareness of being the **mountain – a metaphor for 'settledness'**. Participants were asked to reflect on this feeling and from here looked at the issues they had described in the morning sessions for any change in feeling. The exercise was aimed at regaining control by relaxing, not tensing. The facilitator was using words like 'soft', 'relaxed' and 'cooling' to evoke positive feelings and avoided words that call for action, strength or strain.

Finally, the day ended with a second **guided relaxation**. This time the participants repeated the **body scanning** activity and were asked to notice any difference from the start of the day. The final task of the day was for participants to write down what they want to remember about the day and to share those thoughts within small groups and then with everyone.

4.1.2 Workshop Two – 'Mythodrama'

Workshop Two, 'Mythodrama', was a more collaborative approach, primarily in the form of group work and at times was facilitator directed, for example, in the presentation of particular leadership theories (Table 4.2). It was evident that not all of the issues explored were relevant to the participants' individual circumstances, and therefore, at times, the level of interaction was reduced. 'Mythodrama' was originally developed by Richard Olivier in 1997, who was involved, at that time, with many leading organisations in the UK (for example, GlaxoSmithKline, Deloitte, Microsoft), and he had reported significant success with the approach. Olivier and Verity (2008) explain that the 'mytho' comes from the great stories, and insights into human nature and the 'drama' is enabling the impactful, real learning experience. This became Workshop Two.

The workshop was facilitated by Phyllida Hancock who is a workshop designer and facilitator on leadership and organisational development. After graduating from Cambridge University, Phyllida worked as an actress and singer for 12 years in theatre and on television. Since 2003, she has been an Associate of Olivier Mythodrama and works as a Teaching Associate at Warwick Business School.

The workshop started with an **introduction** by the facilitator, participants and the case study – Shakespeare's play 'As You Like It' (Table 4.3). Then, the participants witnessed the sole **performance of the play** by the facilitator. The facilitator periodically stepped out of his role,

Table 4.2 Structure of Workshop Two: 'Mythodrama'

Approximate timing (min)	Activity	Description
25	Introductions and setting the scene	Facilitator-led introduction to the session.
55	'As You Like It' performance	Facilitator telling the story and enacting the key scenes.
40	'Attunement-achievement' exercise	Group reflection was initiated. No references were made to gender, leadership or the participants' professional or personal concerns or interests.
45	Lunch break	Informal conversations between participants, facilitator and researcher.
20	Picking up the sword: finding sense of self	Facilitator-led reflection activity based on finding a sense of self, followed by a self-facilitated conversation with other participants to consider common experiences.
120	Reflection activity: potential for change	Facilitator-led discussion focussed on behaviours of 'self' and the potential for change.
50	Consideration of 'sticky issues'	Participants were asked to work in two groups on a 'sticky issue'.
15	Wrap up	Reflection on the day, forward planning and lessons learnt.

Table 4.3 Themes in 'As You Like It'

Act I	• Hierarchy and tradition
	• The unendurable present
	• Humour and honest speaking
Act II	• The journey into the unknown
	• Disguises and costumes
	• Surviving in inhospitable territory
Act III	• Building community and finding common ground
	• New life and new voices
	• Learning environments
Act IV	• Educating the heart
	• Forgiveness and redemption
	• Loss of innocence
Act V	• Faith and transformation
	• Making it happen
	• Commitment to the future

Source: Olivier 'Mythodrama' materials.

to pose a question and facilitate dialogue with the participants, ensuring that participants were engaged and checking their understanding of the story. Attention was thus drawn to two settings described in the play: The Court, where people need to keep in line, do not challenge the authority and there is a perceived fear of what is outside the walls; and The Forest: a collective space where everyone is accepted as they are. The environment is uncertain, complex, volatile and ambiguous yet people are expected to behave according to the rules of the palace and gender. The characters are faced with 'wicked problems' that they cannot really solve on their own. The idea or gendered roles and (un)acceptable behaviours is woven in the play and is a key feature of this piece (Gay, 1994).

In the next exercise, participants were asked to recognise the behaviours of 'self' and 'others'. The facilitator introduced an **'attunement-achievement' exercise** inspired by the work of Otto Scharmer (2007) and linked it to aspects of the play. Specifically, the facilitator noted the following points: there are limitations of working in silos, we are all in it together so we need to tune in and it is important to respect different opinions and appreciate others for their contribution. The participants then discussed the differences in the two worlds, which were metaphorically presented in a play as the Court (oppression, hierarchy, how the leadership functions here to keep people alive?) and the Forest (acceptance, collaboration, community, but are there any problems here? why can't we manage to solve, what are the difficulties?). Participants were also asked to consider how they relate their experiences of organisations to the 'As You Like It' story, in particular:

- Relating to the metaphors, seeing parallels (for example: dress-uniform, work/home being two worlds);
- Noticing/judging behaviours not a person;
- Being careful of their own assumptions;
- Reflection on own (the individual participant's) behaviour;
- How do we use our identity to get authority or to be heard.

This session was followed up by a facilitator-led activity based on finding a **sense of self** and conversations with other participants to consider common experiences. To embody the experience, participants were using a **symbolic sword** (wooden stick) to pass around in a circle – each individual took it in turn to speak.

Next, the facilitator proposed a discussion around recognising behaviours of **'self' and the potential for change**, followed by self-facilitated letter writing to the future self and sharing it with one other participant. A facilitator-led career journey model was shared with participants and the opportunity to consider moderating or changing behaviours.

In the last session, participants were asked to work in two groups on a **'sticky issue'**. The idea was based on the discussions at this point in the workshop relating to what wise remedies could individuals bring to the 'sticky issues'. The participants were split into two groups and presented with four 'sticky issue' topics to choose from: 'fear of change, rebellion and cynicism'; 'bias, conflict, and bullying'; 'lack of progress, nothing gets done, and frustration'; and 'living with uncertainty, and disillusionment'. The two groups were asked to work together, with flip charts and pens, to consider: 'what do I need to do differently, what actions do I take?'. The 'sticky issues' chosen for this exercise were 'living with uncertainty' and 'fear of change'.

The final task for the day was to prepare **personal commitments** for the future and present them to the whole group. Participants also had the opportunity to provide feedback about their experiences of the day.

4.2 Insights from the Workshops and Post-workshop Interviews

Women from both workshops appreciated the openness and transparency of the teaching and learning environment and the camaraderie in the women-only environment. This experience had offered them an opportunity to discuss a sensitive topic in a 'safe space' away from their organisational cultures and had increased their awareness of gendered behaviours in the workplace, across all sectors. The women had identified that the development of the life-grid template pre-workshop and a post-workshop follow-up discussion had been a valuable and a unique opportunity to enhance their learning allowing for additional reflection. The women identified a level of discomfort in some of the workshop activities that had led them to be less than fully engaged at times. A contributing factor may be that one of the activities had challenged the gender norms associated with women, another had challenged women's revised gender norms of masculine leadership behaviours, whereas another was felt not relevant to their current circumstances.

Our analysis of the workshops as well as interviews conducted with the participants after their experience in the sessions indicates that the workshop design created a learning environment that was a safe place to explore gender and triggered self-developed learning which was focussed on learning primarily associated with sense-making and reflexive practice. Participants understood the emotional impact of gendered behaviours and the sensory feelings and emotions associated with those organisational behaviours. The workshops also helped them to face gender stereotype threats in the workplace.

4.2.1 Creating a Safe Place to Explore Gender

All of the women's narratives described the learning environment as a significant influence on their experiences, portraying it as a safe space to explore gender: *'there was a great deal of immediate trust in there'* [Professional 17]. For less experienced managers it was an anxious start: *'I felt like a duck out of water'* [Professional 15], but it was short lived as the commonality of gender experiences became apparent: *'just listening to the same issues, the same way they felt, it was like wow'* [Professional 19]. Many narratives revealed an increased awareness of gender facilitated by the workshops and research process. For some, this awareness developed from listening to the experiences of other participants: *'I've been able to reflect on other people's experience in a way that I can use'* [Professional 15]. For others, it was insightful to hear different dynamics across many sectors: *'I think when you have worked in one sector for a long time, you can get quite insular'* [Professional 17]. The narratives also contained a sense of a new awareness that gender experiences were not isolated to a particular field. Julie's words are representative:

> people were from very different backgrounds, very different jobs, but we were all experiencing much the same things going on at work, and the dilemmas that we had.
>
> [Professional 8]

The sharing of gender issues had created a sense of comfort, an attachment to others': *'it was like an invisible connection between us all, it was unspoken, but was felt'* [Professional 16]. This sense of comfort provided many participants with a safe environment away from the office to share and discuss experiences that they feared would be negatively judged in their working environments. For Angela, this experience was related to interpersonal hostility:

> who else would I talk to about it? [...] you don't want to broadcast the fact that in previous work roles people have taken a dislike to you, because others will wonder why? [...]. So you don't broadcast it for fear that it's going to reflect on you.
>
> [Professional 1]

For others, it was related to their cultural environment:

> *there was a sense of actually, it doesn't matter if I get it wrong, or say something I shouldn't say. [...]. If I said something a little bit inappropriate or contentious, it was alright, because I wouldn't be judged.*

[Professional 17]

> *I really enjoyed being in a session where it was all women. I don't think I've ever done that before, so it was quite refreshing [...], and it was much more comfortable and relaxed [...]. There were no egos.*

[Professional 14]

The camaraderie provided many participants with a sense of 'it's not just me', but that was tinged with disappointment:

> *my experiences are more common than I knew or believed, just because we are so protective of ourselves, and frightened of being judged [...]. I don't think I was pleased, because I don't think I want everyone to go through those experiences, but it was just a surprise.*

[Professional 16]

This feeling of disappointment was echoed in many narratives, as awareness of the scale and impact of gender in the workplace became apparent. Veronica's words are representative as she spoke about a fellow participant:

> *I really noticed the way it made her feel when she was talking, she was getting quite upset, I was quite surprised. Another strong women, but someone was really, really affecting her that much [...] I could really relate.*

[Professional 19]

It confirmed for a few participants what they believed to be true:

> *things haven't changed. We like to believe that we fought a fight and we won and things have improved, but I would question [...] have they changed? I don't think they have.*

[Professional 10]

4.2.2 Self-developed Learning

All of the post-workshop narratives contained elements of self-developed learning primarily associated with the techniques of sense-making and reflexive practice. The learning portrayed clarity of thought for many participants, and this was particularly evident in the participants' narratives of those who had participated in Workshop Two – 'Mythodrama'. The play 'As You Like It' was placed in the context of a world that was 'volatile, uncertain, complex and ambiguous'. All participants listened intently throughout the play. Post-workshop narratives confirmed a high level of engagement: *'that wonderful storytelling way of doing it has stuck in my mind'* [Professional 2]; *'I loved the story, absolutely loved the story'* [Professional 1]. At the end of the performance, participants were asked for their reactions and interpretations of the story. The facilitator made no reference to gender, leadership or the participant's professional or personal concerns or interests.

The performance had stimulated a variety of thoughts. Some participants considered themselves in the multiple roles played out in organisational life: *'I could see times when I had taken on a number of the characters both male and female'* [Professional 12]. Others aligned the players within the story to individuals within their organisations: *'even some of the trickier characters in the play [...] you could see where they were coming from'* [Professional 14]. A few recognised a potentially different approach: *'leaders who show vulnerability are more captivating and engaging'*.

On the other hand, Workshop One, 'Sense-making', offered a sensory engagement with the body and one's feelings created by the difficult situations. Workshop One allowed participants to examine themselves, their feelings and thoughts and share these aspects through metaphorical lenses. It showed both esteem building and calming techniques to help in dealing with gender threat. The facilitator was clearly aiming at reframing the negative experience and reactionism into positive proactive and confident actions.

To illustrate self-developed learning further, we now share two vignettes: one from each workshop. Both narratives portray the judgement of others. For Linda [Workshop Two], the sense-making resulted in a change to her own behaviour and removed the negative judgement she held of other's (Vignette 6). For Justine [Workshop One], the self-developed learning was related to her own behaviour only (Vignette 7). Linda and Justine's stories are detailed further in Appendix 1 (Case Studies 3 and 5), respectively.

Vignette 6   Removal of Negative Judgement of Other's

In her pre-workshop interview, Linda had described a strained relationship with her line manager, who she believed was blocking her career progression. Her line manager was being told what to do by a senior male officer, and she had obeyed as expected, in her male-dominated environment. Linda had perceived a lack of fit between her line manager's actions and the equality values of the organisation. She had felt a complete lack of support from her line manager, something that Linda would not do to her own staff. She had felt she could 'fight the good fight', 'be strong' and 'stand up', but sometimes she got tired of being the one: '*it would be nice to have an easy life*'. In her post-workshop interview, Linda had altered the way she perceived and engaged with a situation described pre-workshop. She had reflected on her own feelings of frustration with her line manager and how that may be perceived by others: '*I was so hacked off, I wonder if that's reflected in how I'm behaving at work [...] how I am with others*'? She had also recognised that the behaviour displayed by her manager was not in her 'normal' character, prompting Linda to reconsider other factors that may be impacting on her, for example, the ongoing restructuring of the organisation: '*she may be in a worse place than me*'. Linda saw this as new behaviour for her: '*I feel better equipped*' [to deal with this situation].

[Professional 14]

The interpretation we place on this finding is that Linda had been able to think deeply about the situation. She had moved away from the bias assumptions she had taken for granted. She was focussed on seeing the world differently: '*it is time to regenerate, and to think about my behaviour towards others*'.

Vignette 7   Awareness of Own Behaviours

In her photographs, Justine used a sign displaying the words: '*feed me non-recyclable waste only please*' to represent her line manager: '*going over the same thing, again, and again, and again*' [her inference being the performance targets]; a soft leather seat represented her feelings of: '*darkness and uncomfortableness*'.

Justine remembered many of her photographs in the post-work-shop interview, in particular, referenced the rubbish bins and a fire escape sign. They had made a significant impression on her. The picture of the rubbish bins came to represent the experience of: '*varying degrees of rubbish*'. She confirmed that the colours of the bins represented her feelings: '*the hurt*' [orange], and '*the calm in her mind*' [blue]. The fire escape sign came to represent '*man taking me down, [...], it was a dark sort of roller coaster*'.

In the post-workshop interview, Justine had retained the same language and a sense of anger, as she described her ex-line manager: '*it's like I'm looking at him as some sort of puppet, I can almost see the strings, I can almost see the strings*'. She had held onto the negative judgement of her ex-boss. The workshop had no impact on this situation. However, Justine's post-workshop transcript exposes a greater level of self-control that she described as 'orange polished steel': '*There is an orange brightness and that polished steel is something a little bit more refined than it was before*'.

[Professional 7]

The interpretation we place on this description is that the metaphors used in the workshop confirmed her pre-workshop feelings towards others, and she had subsequently used the tool of a metaphor to affirm a level of self-control. Through the experience, she had recognised a need to be 'a little bit more refined', protecting herself from the perceived threat and the consequence of failure.

4.2.3 The Emotional Impact of Gendered Behaviours

The emotional impact of gendered behaviours is demonstrated throughout the narratives. However, the constructivist nature of Workshop One allowed participants to construct their own knowledge related to an issue of choice. The issue was set in the context of their individual 'fit' within their current organisational culture. All issues identified were arguably gendered and fell broadly into three categories: relationships with other colleagues, male-dominated organisational cultures and performance and effectiveness. The participants were guided through a process to create a poem, representing their sensory feelings towards the core issue. Three participants used words that described annoyance and frustration: '*quite hard, rigid, dark, hot, contracted, boiling, bubbling*'. Four described feelings of restraint and suppression: '*tight, knotted, suffocation or lack of air, cold and tethered*'; '*I feel really heavy and anchored, at the bottom, the energy is very tight, my head is very bubbly, and it's almost as if I'm frightened to let the light shine, so as you constrain this energy that needs to come out, you feel really heavy*' [Professional 16]. One participant described a need to conceal any display of emotion in their situation:

> *my heart is pumping and I feel red [...] almost like a bottle of champagne that they are shaking [...], but I have to keep the lid on [...]. There's a certain professionalism that is required.*
>
> [Professional 8]

For a few participants, there was a distinct change in the tone of their voices as they described feeling vulnerable and anxious: '*my head is busy and buzzing [...]. It's not painful, but you almost feel a bit nauseous with it. I speak to a lot of women, and a lot of women get this feeling*' [Professional 9].

Participants chose eight sensory words from their initial list to form the basis of a poem. Many poems were incredibly poignant. Christine's poem is representative, describing the sensory feeling of being in a male-dominated environment:

> *I feel tight, try as I might,*
> *Can't get it right, dark as night,*
> *I'm mumbling, feel I'm stumbling, fumbling,*
> *Can't stop the bubbling,*
> *A single digit, small, invisible midget,*
> *I feel rigid.*
>
> [Professional 4]

Participants took photographs to represent or activate the same sensory feeling (Table 4.4). The feelings most commonly shared were 'anger', 'suffocation', 'tenseness', 'vulnerability' and 'uncomfortableness'. Table 4.4 displays a selection of the images taken and includes indicative extracts from the nine texts.

4.2.4 Facing the Gender Stereotype Threat

Many of the women's post-workshop narratives confirmed reduction or mediation in gender stereotype threat falling into two broad categories. Firstly, 'reaffirmation of self-worth' revealed that women had increased personal values both during the arts-based workshop and post-workshop. Secondly, increased 'self-efficacy' revealed that women

Table 4.4 Selected images representing emotions linked to gendered behaviours

Image	Sensory feeling
 *Image 1* Fire extinguisher	*'representing the heat that I feel'* [Professional 18] *'it takes away air and resonates with suffocation'* [Professional 10] *'I get really angry and just annoyed'* [Professional 8]
 *Image 2* Lock	*'just being locked away with regards to your spirit. Sometimes I feel your spirit is not allowed to break free'* [Professional 16]
 *Image 3* Rubbish bins	*'feeling of being in the dark and it's difficult to get out'* [Professional 10] *'the hurt (orange), the calm in my mind (blue)'* [Professional 7]

(taken from Workshop One: Sense-making with associated quotes)

had increased belief and in some cases could demonstrate their action to resolve a gendered situation. These two findings are discussed in the next sections.

4.2.4.1 Reaffirmation of Self-worth

To illustrate the reaffirmation of self-worth, we share three narratives in more detail, chosen for specific reasons. For Christine, sensory experience of Workshop One generated new feelings and developed further understanding of the problem (Vignette 8). For Angela and Colleen, Workshop Two had clarified their current situation, and had generated specific action in the workshop itself (Vignettes 9 and 10, respectively).

Vignette 8 Self-worth and New Feelings

Christine was the only woman of 50 employees in a private sector organisation owned by herself and her business partner. She felt that her male colleagues viewed her as 'the office girl'. During the workshop, she took photographs to represent what she was feeling. One photograph was recalled in the post-workshop interview that had made a particularly strong impression on her. It was one coffee cup on a table.

Image 4 Solitary cup on a table (Vignette 8)

This cup came to signify the experience of feeling like: '*a solitary discarded object*'. Christine spoke with an emotional voice in the workshop as she described being surprised at the anger she was feeling: '*I'm quite shaky, just being forced to focus on it*'. Clearly,

---

considering this aspect was new for her. In her post-workshop narrative, Christine developed this understanding further. Her insight of the situation was changing, and was visible in the strength and forcefulness of her words, as she described insisting that there was a change, despite resistance from her business partner: '*I don't have to stay in this environment that's annoying me, so I've kind of removed myself from the situation somewhat [...] which I wanted to do, but this* [referring to the workshop] *made me do it sooner than I would have otherwise. It has become much more bearable*' [Professional 4].

Using the picture of a solitary cup on a table as a metaphor for the difficult situation allowed Christine to move away from seeing the situation as something about her being perceived as an 'office girl', to seeing the problem in terms of anger and loneliness. With this new perception, her feelings about the problematic situation were confirmed.

The new metaphor brought her feelings to the fore, which she responded to by 'disengaging' from the situation. The disengagement was an adaptive response from Christine that had allowed her to maintain a positive self-view, maintain motivation and her persistence which, within a limited or context-specific situation, is healthy and protective.

Vignette 9 Increased Clarity of Feelings

Angela's narrative describes a difficult and stressful time in her early career. She portrays a significant lack of confidence in her ability, believing others' to be 'smarter' than her. Angela considered herself to be a follower, rather than a leader, despite her transcripts containing many examples of her leadership. She attributed this self-doubt to fear of showing weakness as a woman: '*I have that little immediate panic, and then go right, deep breath, let's get on with it*'. If she failed, she would prove the weakness in women to be true.

In the workshop, Angela had rehearsed a 'different version of herself' with her fellow participants. They had been impressed by her 'performance', and she had received several compliments. This had an unexpected impact on Angela. In the following exercise, she surprised herself by volunteering to take a lead. She credited this to her own acceptance of being 'equally capable' in a workshop environment: '*it was realisation for me, [...]. I was happy to take the lead [...], and comfortable doing so*'. This experience was new for her. In her post-workshop narrative, she portrays an increased confidence. Angela gave an example of her new approach in the delivery of a public presentation: '*this is the first time that I wasn't shaking [...]. I didn't even need my notes, I believed in what I was saying*'.

[Professional 1]

Angela had felt safe and supported in the learning environment to explore her life experiences of being judged by others. She had moved away from her bias of others and was able to control her feelings in a situation in which she would have previously felt vulnerable.

Vignette 10 Increased Clarity of Own Behaviour

Colleen had been successful in her career, rising to a position of Director. She had enjoyed this work, but after eight years, she was made redundant. For the next two years, she had temporary roles, before finally securing a permanent position in the public sector. She was grateful for the opportunity, despite feeling disappointed that the position had a lower level of seniority than her previous position.

Colleen's narrative displays agentic behaviours, for example, using direct dialogue with her Chief Executive to share her views and challenge his thoughts. She believed that her male colleagues were 'shocked' at her approach, and she had often used humour to lighten the situation. In doing so, she felt her male colleagues did not take her seriously, which had impacted on her career progression. During the workshop, Colleen had recognised that she needed to act. Her post-workshop transcript describes a more 'professional' approach, she explains:

I had to do a presentation [...]. I thought actually I'm going to do this properly and seriously. I actually stopped myself doing the one liner at the beginning [...], so it was just that kind of playing it straight bat.

Colleen had also reflected on her vision of possible futures. Despite a few reservations about her current organisation, it seemed she was preparing herself to pursue her career on this path. Since the workshop, Colleen had been clear with others of her career ambitions: *'I've been more able to say [...] I want to lead that, without adding "is that all right"? Just doing it more confidently, [...] I'm getting the work, and getting the opportunities'*.

[Professional 3]

Colleen had reflected on her previous director experience and, through access to reflective space, had increased consciousness of her current style, from her own point of view, and had taken specific action to enhance her career opportunities. She had moved away from her bias towards her male colleagues, looking further into the future.

4.2.4.2 Increased Self-efficacy

The second area of gender stereotype threat reduction or mediation is increased self-efficacy. Increased self-efficacy was highlighted in many texts post-workshop: *'the biggest thing I would say I've improved [...] I've felt far more confident in myself, and in my role, and in my opinions'* [Professional 7]. To illustrate increased self-efficacy further, we share two vignettes in more detail (11 and 12, respectively), which were chosen for a specific reason. When we met Jennifer and Valerie post-workshop, it was clear that the workshop experience had a profound effect upon them: *'I think about my mountain a lot. I've told everybody who would benefit from it'* [Professional 9]. In their post-workshop narratives, they had recognised an increased self-efficacy that they both attributed to the sensory experiences of Workshop One – 'Sense-making'.

Vignette 11 Increased Self-efficacy through Metaphor

Jennifer had been 'headhunted' to chair a prestigious community development board in a town where she ran her beauty business. Jennifer perceived she lacked ability to take on her new role: *'I ain't got the skills to do this, I haven't got the vocabulary [...]. I don't know how to chair a meeting'*. She had known they had wanted her for the position, and she did not want to let them down: *'I've been*

Image 5 An emergency exit sign (Vignette 11)

pulled in to do this role, they want me to do this role, and [...] I want to make it right for everybody else'. She had self-imposed standards for meeting preparation: *'I would study it* [the board reports], *I would have the numbers, I would have it like that'* [indicating very precise]. Jennifer was working many hours to meet her self-imposed targets, and the situation was making her feel 'vulnerable and anxious'. In the workshop, Jennifer took various photographs to express her sensory experience of the problem. An emergency exit sign, to illustrate: *'racing against both herself and time'*.

Interestingly, she had also recognised that this state was not sustainable. She took a photograph of a damaged car, to illustrate her raised awareness of the situation: *'I think we can crash, if we're not careful'*. In the post-workshop narrative, Jennifer portrayed her approach to a recent board meeting. She had experienced the meeting differently, and her tone of voice shared the excitement. Jennifer had felt more confident and had not spent as much time preparing for the meeting. She also described that she had felt that board members put 'a bomb' on her mountain during the meeting. She depicts her sense of calmness in the situation, a feeling that was unusual for her. She attributed this new feeling to the sensory experience of the workshop: *'understanding the word confidence, [...] as an emotion [...], not letting people chip at it, or rain on it, or snow on it* [referring to the mountain]. *It can do that, but the centre of that mountain is solid and holding onto that, you are who you are'*.

[Professional 9]

Jennifer confirmed that she had thought about the 'solidness' of the mountain many times since the workshop, and this new understanding of confidence had been insightful for her. She was certain that the new feeling was sustainable: '*you can't remember the words, but I can always remember a happy time [...] it resonated with me [...] and that's something I can carry around*' [Professional 9]. The term of her role as chair was coming up soon after the workshop. Pre-workshop, Jennifer was adamant she was not interested in continuing in the role, but her feelings had changed. She had an increased self-belief and inner strength to continue in her current professional identity. There is more on Jennifer in Appendix 1 (Case Study 1).

Vignette 12 Increased Self-efficacy through Sensory Engagement

Valerie was a Head of Service in a public sector organisation and had recently taken on a new role. In her view, one aspect of the service she had recently acquired should be the responsibility of another department. This was her core problem as the conversation

Image 6 Window (Vignette 12)

---

was at an impasse. It was clear that Valerie was frustrated by this situation as she had clarity of the proposed change in her own mind but was having difficulty in persuading her male colleagues to agree with her view. Valerie found sensory words to describe the problem:

> *I feel three different things [...] I'm clear in my head, but it feels really prickly. I go into the conversations irritated, but it's that prickly feeling that they are not getting it, but then my legs are like jelly because they are there, they are wiser, they have been in the organisation longer [...] my heads absolutely clear, but inside, the middle bit, I feel sick.*

She took photographs to represent what she was feeling. One picture represented her new understanding of the situation: the image of a window.

This picture came to represent the experience of feeling tense but also a clearness of thinking: '*the jelly that I had in the legs, the pink bit is cherry jelly, and the white is the kind of clarity, the whiteness in my head, in the conversations*'. She also used the image

Image 7 Books on a shelf (Vignette 12)

of a bookshelf to represent her desire to regain control of the situation: '*everything is in order* [in the image]. *This situation is not in order*'.

Valerie spoke enthusiastically in the workshop as she described her surprise at her ability to pinpoint the feelings associated with meeting her colleagues: '*anxious, knotty type of feeling*'. Clearly, considering this aspect was new for her.

In her post-workshop narrative, Valerie described this realisation as a 'big learning'. For the first time, she had been able to break her issue down into three parts. This had given her insight, and she reviewed her approach to the situation. Valerie explained how she had prepared a handover plan, approaching her two male colleagues with increased confidence. They had accepted the plan without question.

[Professional 18]

Valerie had moved away from seeing the situation as something that was 'irritating' to seeing the problem in terms of her own 'self-doubt and anxiousness'. The new metaphor created had brought her feelings to the fore, which she responded to by approaching the situation in a more positive manner, keeping control of her feelings. She had felt that this experience was quite profound, and she had reflected on it many times since the workshop.

4.3 Evaluation and Room for Improvement

Our critical position has been to evaluate specific modes of arts-based methods against a specific purpose of the perceptions and moderators of gender stereotype threat. The evaluation of those specific modes confirmed that:

- an individualised approach of sensory engagement through the use of poetry, photography and 'metaphor' focussed on a personalised gendered issue can moderate gender stereotype threat by increasing women's positive self-view and self-belief;
- for some women, being 'placed' in the gender stereotype threatening domain led to confirmation of old impressions, rather than creating new ones, resulting in little change to the identified gender stereotype threat;

- relying on individuals' engagement in the observation of behaviours through the performance of a play did not specifically lead to moderate gender stereotype threat. However, it did stimulate sense-making leading to self-development, including clarity of thought about how individuals consider their own position, the roles of others, and their interaction with others in the workplace;
- a facilitated approach involving the presentation of leadership theories did not specifically lead to moderation of the impact of gender stereotype threat; and
- spending time with a personal gendered experience, without immediately reflecting upon it, had a more immediate and tangible outcome than pure sense-making where the learning tended to be more hypothetical in nature.

There was an overwhelming positive feedback on both workshops. However, the post-workshop interviews revealed three aspects of the workshops that made only modest impressions on participants who viewed them as challenging activities or which were not relevant to them.

Firstly, in Workshop One, participants were asked to move into groups of three to explore the sense of 'settledness'. Each would speak for five minutes about a time when they had felt 'settledness', describing how it feels in the body, whereas the other two would listen. Those listening were asked to be 'rooted and relaxed' like a mountain, and not react in any way, constraining facial expressions. In the narratives, all participants expressed their uncomfortableness with this exercise, which they felt was quite emotional: *'it's very personal, so it was very difficult. I would find it much easier to talk to a mirror in a room for myself'* [Professional 18]. The post-workshop interview illuminated the discomfort further. For a few, the uncomfortableness was in talking about themselves: *'it's hard to say I can do this, and I can do that, I find this really hard'* [Professional 19]. For others, it was the inability to display reassurance to those speaking: *'the difficulty I found was not responding […] you always want to nod, smile and encourage someone'* [Professional 7]. For some, it was the lack of receiving encouragement: *'I found that really difficult […] it's all about getting that recognition through a conversation that someone's listening to you and interested in what you're having to say'* [Professional 9]. Two had felt it got more comfortable as the exercise progressed: *'the first minute was quite uncomfortable […] the second one didn't feel as bad […] by the third*

[…] it seemed fine' [Professional 4]. Our observation of this exercise was that participants had found it a difficult exercise, and there was a sense of discomfort. Participants were concentrating intensely on each other during this exercise: *'some were smiling, but there was a lot of "un-emotion"'*. Participants were whispering, which was a change of mood from the earlier perception. One group was just reflecting, rather than speaking: *'silences were appearing'*. We overheard one participant say: *'this is going to go down well in the workplace'*. The others in the group laughed.

Secondly, in Workshop Two, participants were asked to consider: *'when is the time for gentleness and compassion, and when do you need your swords?'*. The inference being that the sword was representing something that was not 'gentleness and compassion'. Most participants described aspects of performance and effectiveness, self-confidence and self-belief, for example, 'professional expertise', 'drive and motivation'. Two participants believed that the sword had represented relationships with others. The second part of this exercise was to imagine making an entrance onto the stage as a different version of yourself, i.e. putting down the sword. Participants shared this new version of themselves with another participant. At the end of this exercise, participants were given an opportunity to retain their sword or leave it on the ground. Nine of the ten women chose to retain their sword. Post-workshop narratives confirmed that two participants had only a vague recollection of this exercise: *'I remember picking the sword back up. I can't remember what I was saying'* [Professional 14]. Five participants confirmed that they would continue to hold onto their sword, whereas for some the use of the sword had increased since the workshop: *'I've had to use my sword even more […]. I realised that for now, it's really important that I have it, because if I'm not motivated and I'm not driven, it will be hard for the team'* [Professional 12]. In effect, only one participant planned to make a new entrance.

Thirdly, in Workshop 2 participants were asked to choose a 'sticky issue' to work on in groups. The topics chosen were 'living with uncertainty' and 'fear of change'. The post-workshop narratives confirmed that only one participant had connected with this exercise, which was in her professional field. Five participants had felt no association with the chosen topic: *'I would never have picked that topic, I went with the majority really because I felt that some of them had some really good stuff to say'* [Professional 11]; *'I do remember it, but I didn't feel it at that moment. It's not an issue every day'* [Professional 3]. For two participants, it was an interesting conversation about managing change: '*it was quite a supportive conversation, we probably went a bit off topic, and talked about how you cope with change*' [Professional 14]. One felt that the change model presented was idealistic: '*in reality, it's as far from the truth as you could probably get. That's speaking from experience at the moment*' [Professional 12].

5   Moving Forward
Gender, Arts-Based Interventions and Coaching

In this chapter, we demonstrate that the vicious circle of gender stereotype fulfilment and propagation set in motion by gender stereotype activation can be broken through an individualised arts-based coaching approach. We strongly believe that this approach can moderate gender stereotype threat by increasing women's positive self-view and self-belief to give professional women the opportunity to address the organisational realities they face at any given time adequately. From our highly qualified and experienced coaching backgrounds, we have found that an individualised arts-based coaching approach has stimulated fresh insight into our creative coaching by adapting the learning from the research and building it into our coaching practice. This has been invaluable in looking for new ways of developing increased awareness from a coach and coachee perspective, focussed on the concept of 'the self' and 'others' within the context of a real-life situation.

A significant amount of research has been devoted to examining the effects of gender stereotype threat on activation, and it has been proven that gender stereotype threat has been reduced or eliminated (Davies et al., 2005) by involving 'the self' (Wheeler et al., 2007), by thinking about characteristics in the threatened domain (Rosenthal et al., 2007) and by encouraging self-affirmation (Cohen et al., 2006). Much research to date has focussed on a scientific approach involving 'priming' or 'non-priming' of women (a technique whereby exposure to one stimulus influences a response to a subsequent stimulus, without conscious guidance or intention (Davies et al., 2005). Our approach was to ensure that the development of new theory was set in a 'real-life' and current situation, aligning with the ideals of self-awareness, self-control and self-realisation (Edwards et al., 2013), which is promoted by many arts-based methods and coaching techniques. Indeed, Aviv (2014, p. 1) contends that:

abstract art frees our brain from the dominance of reality, enabling it to flow within its inner states, create new emotional and cognitive associations, and activate brain-states that are otherwise harder to access.

According to Taylor and Ladkin (2009), the increased use of these non-cognitive methods (processes of acquiring knowledge through the senses, experience or reasoning) enables individuals to access perceptions, feelings, stories, creativity, awareness in the moment and empathy, all of which contribute to a wider appreciation of leadership in, and of, organisations and of oneself. It proactively engages individuals in motivated and purposeful acts, taking specific action to shape and sustain and co-construct their identities in a diverse context that may serve to challenge the complexities and create possibilities in a gendered work environment (Roberts and Creary, 2013). According to Eisner (2004), in the absence of rules, art teaches us to appraise the consequences of one's choices, and to revise and then to make other choices, with the potential to view stereotypical behaviours and subsequent actions in a more positive way, both for 'self' and 'others', for example, to confront non-rational decision-making. Before we move onto positive psychology in coaching, we would like to spend a little time on the concept of 'self' and 'others' that formed the basis of our arts-based approach and links directly to our individualised coaching approach.

5.1 The Concept of 'Self' and 'Others'

The concept of 'self' and 'others' lies within a symbolic interactionist perspective, a framework that locates 'the self' as a crucial element in the analysis of social behaviour, with identity dependent upon seeking self-meaning and control of action (Cassell and Symon, 1994). Through a process of interaction and communication with others, the individual responds to others and adjusts his or her understanding and behaviour, as a shared sense of order and reality that is 'negotiated' with others. Central to the process is the notion that people continually change in the light of social circumstances, and that the individual's sense of identity is constantly being constructed and reconstructed (Saunders et al., 2012). Navigating 'self' is an emergent, interpretive process of 'becoming' (Cunliffe, 2004), inferring individual empowerment, a bottom-up approach that proactively engages individuals in motivated and purposeful acts, taking specific action to shape and sustain their own identity that may serve to challenge the complexities and create possibilities in a gendered work environment (Roberts and Creary, 2013). Tactics for navigating 'the self' generally seek to identify pathways for cultivating more positive identities in diverse work settings to fulfil individual needs including recognition, control and purpose. It reflects how an individual develops a self-understanding that is coherent, distinct and positively valued within the context of complex, ambiguous and contradictory experiences, described by Snow and Anderson (1987, p. 1348) as 'the range of activities individuals engage in to create, present, and sustain personal identities that are congruent with, and supportive of the self-concept'.

The process captures an individual's storied self-understanding, placing an emphasis on sense-making for navigating 'the self', situated in 'the past' (who they have been), 'the present' (who they are) and 'the future' (who they are becoming) (Roberts and Creary, 2013). Theorists in this area claim that proactively investigating behavioural practices can influence the significance and meaning of identities in diverse work contexts.

> It is the formal conceptualisation of the ways in which human beings are "being continuously engaged in forming, repairing, maintaining, strengthening or revising the constructions that are productive of a sense of coherence and distinctiveness."
>
> (Sveningsson and Alvesson, 2003, p. 1165)

Ambady et al. (2004) confirmed that differentiating individuals from one another by focussing on 'the self' is a protective measure against the detrimental effects of negative gender stereotype activation. Building on this notion, Roberts and Creary (2013) suggested that navigating 'the self' can actively engage individuals in shaping, and sustaining their own identity, which may serve well to challenge the complexities in a gendered work environment. In parallel to this notion, the contemporary developments within arts-based methods and coaching have drawn on a variety of theoretical perspectives that all highlight the significance of 'self' and 'others'. Tactics for navigating 'the self' generally seek to identify pathways for cultivating more positive identities in diverse work settings to fulfil individual needs including recognition, control and purpose. This is fundamentally what women are seeking when they 'feel' gender stereotype threat. In the next section, we specifically link the theory of arts-based methods used in our research to that of our coaching approach within the framework of positive psychology in coaching discussed further in Section 5.3.

5.2 From Workshops and Interviews to Coaching Interventions

In the interviews and workshops, the facilitators led the professional women through a process of enquiry, learning and action. The interviews and workshops, like any form of coaching, aimed to help the professional women towards a desirable outcome – an objective. The approach taken in the interviews and workshops, and in our coaching practice, is based on a belief of the ability of the individual to move their own situation forward. Basically, it aims to help coachees find the courage, energy, hope and perseverance necessary to reach their desired goals. As coaches, we know how transformative the coaching experience can be for coachees as we believe that each person holds so much power within herself. At times, individuals just need a little nudge, direction or support to allow great things to happen.

To promote this approach, we use advanced skills of listening, questioning and reflection to create a highly effective conversation and/ or experience for the coachee. The workshops and the interviews were not intended to solve the individuals' problems; rather, aligned with a coaching approach, the problems would be 'fixed' through the process itself. This less directive style not only allows individuals to find their own solutions but just as importantly increases their belief that they can surface their own insights and ideas, increasing their sense of engagement in the situation.

A coaching approach provides a development programme that meets professional women's needs in a timely way and addresses the gendered issues identified by the women themselves. This approach gives professional women an opportunity through confidential 'one to one' or peer group conversations to discuss gendered challenges in the workplace and identify solutions to those challenges.

Etymologically, the word 'coaching' comes from the Hungarian town of Kocs where horse drawn carriages were made. By the 19th century, a coach was somebody who was working with athletes to help them improve their performance. Traditionally, that performance with externally set standards was the basis for the agenda driven by a coach who was expected to have expertise in the task at hand. Today's understanding of coaching has moved from a directive approach, which is now closer to today's practice of mentoring, to a more non-directive approach (Bachkirova et al., 2018).

Coaching involves continuous involvement in a cycle of analysing the current situation, seeing potential pathways for resolving problems, setting goals and planning actions to achieve them and has been accepted and valued as a tried and tested means of passing on knowledge, skills and wisdom to other people (Parkin, 2010). Coaching delivers results by providing a supportive environment and a space for reflection (Flaherty,

2010), and in this way, it helps to unlock potential (Whitmore, 2017). We tend to favour the view that coaching should be seen as a flexible technique for personal and/or professional development which is essentially non-directive and has been proven to be effective as a method of motivating and supporting individuals and/or teams to deliver set goals and objectives (Hunt & Fielden, 2016; Bachkirova et al., 2018).

Coe et al. (2008) argue that people who become fully committed to achieve set goals are those who are clear about core values and performance goals, set for, or by them in the first place. The coach's role is to help the coachee formulate appropriate, achievable goals that matter to the coachee and the achievement of which would make a difference for the coachee in terms of their work, career or professional development (Flaherty, 2010) or, indeed, their personal development.

The definition of coaching is one that has been actively explored in the literature with many authors agreeing that coaching is different and distinctive (Passmore et al., 2012), while having areas of overlap with many other interventions – for example, counselling, psychology, learning and consulting. Theoretically, those relationships can be relatively clearly distinguished, whereas the practical delimitations are more tricky and form more of a continuum (Hawkins & Smith, 2006). In our work, we find it particularly difficult to perform coaching without elements of mentoring. Similarly, a few of our coaching interactions revealed that more arts-based methods, positive psychology and some knowledge of counselling techniques and safeguarding protocols were useful.

In summary, as coaches today, we work with individuals to enable them to become more successful in all aspects of their life, by setting and achieving better goals, helping them to prioritise, constructively challenging and realising their potential. In essence, coaching is the art of facilitating another person's learning, development, well-being and performance, closing the gap between their 'current state', their potential and to better prepare them for management or leadership. Before we move onto specific coaching approaches that we have found inspirational and helpful, we would like to place them in the context of positive psychology in coaching.

5.3 Positive Psychology in Coaching

Coaching is one of the fields that can benefit from the science of positive psychology, particularly in relation to work–life and organisations. In many organisations, the science of positive psychology is being applied to improve workplace coaching practices, leadership and organisational development efforts (Passmore et al., 2012).

According to Kauffman et al. (2010, p.158), positive psychology coaching is:

> *a scientifically-rooted approach to helping clients increase well-being, enhance and apply strengths, improve performance, and achieve valued goals. At the core of positive psychology coaching is a belief in the power of science to elucidate the best methods for development.*

Within positive psychology, there are a multitude of tools that can help a coach build a highly tailored, structured coaching journey that is ultimately backed up by measurable evidence. Ultimately, the coach is helping the coachee to develop an understanding of negative thoughts and behaviours versus positive thoughts and behaviours and understanding what is needed to achieve their goals and objectives. Fundamentally, this was our approach in the research workshops.

Passmore et al. (2012) emphasise the distinction between coaching and coaching psychology in that coaching is aimed at relatively healthy individuals, but both coaching and therapy can use established psychological interventions. We believe that an understanding of psychological approaches helps a coach to broaden the scope of techniques and better adapt to individual needs.

In our current thinking, we follow Whitmore (2017, p. 10) and see coaching as 'unlocking people's potential to maximise their own performance. It is helping them to learn rather than teaching them'. As coaching deals with people and their motivations, we see considerable value in psychological approaches to coaching, and coaching literature refers to the plenitude of inspirations from behaviourist, psychodynamic, person centred and cognitive psychology, as well as existential and constructive approaches or even neuroscience (Palmer & Whybrow, 2019).

We found that through reframing and creativity in the arts-based workshops, a 'let's look at it another way approach', the professional women were able to generate ideas, which created lateral or creative thinking, to see the problem in a different, more positive way and to find ways of applying those ideas.

The arts have historical and philosophical roots in psychology based on the basic human need to create, communicate, create coherence and symbolise. According to Jung (1966), art touches and also expresses the whole complex human person, including levels of mind, body and spirit. The humanities connect people across different cultures and traditions to common challenges of the human condition: for example, gender stereotyping. The arts can provide a diagnostic image of culture and the individual while providing access to multiple modes of intelligence, communication and problem-solving. Art connects us to the imagination (McNiff, 1981) and bridges the conscious and unconscious.

In the following sections, we focus on some psychological roots used in our research and in our coaching practice that we have found inspirational and helpful for professional women: narrative and storytelling, metaphor, mindfulness and sensory engagement. We then move onto concluding reflections and end the chapter with our thoughts for the future.

5.4 Narrative and Storytelling

A narrative approach fits with our world view as individuals and professionals stemming from constructive ontology and symbolism. 'Narrative therapy', as it is called in psychological circles, has been used for many years by therapists to encourage individuals to reframe or see a problem differently. Boje (1999) says that people can get on a track of telling the same (often very negative) story endlessly about themselves which, in turn, can become a self-fulfilling prophecy. Although coaching is not therapy, we have found that using this approach can have positive results as the coaching is in a reflective space where the main focus is on values and on providing opportunities for sense-making. Problematic experiences or events are reframed by unfolding alternative narratives: for example, the impact of gender stereotypes. These are based on re-experience and recollection, as well as on the process of co-creation between coach and coachee.

Our research fostered personal and social sense-making through the use of narrative by reframing a situation and building self-esteem and confidence. Specifically, we found that moderation of gender stereotype threat occurred for some individuals both in and following the arts-based workshop where (i) individuals are encouraged to engage in sensory experience of being in the gender stereotype-threatened domain through metaphorical engagement and (ii) individuals are encouraged to think of themselves and others differently in terms of their unique values and characteristics.

Further exploration found that the individualised approach of placing women in a 'real' gender stereotype threat situation had a more significant and immediate impact on moderating gender stereotype threat than simply encouraging women to think of themselves and others differently. The former had allowed women to increase their positive self-view and self-belief and, in many cases, had resulted in a specific action to progress their learning into the future – whereas the latter resulted in learning that was more hypothetical in nature. The women displayed a strong commitment to enact this hypothetical learning post-workshop. However, their description of the learning was relatively superficial and the sustainability of the learning seemed less likely to impact their future behaviours.

In essence, acting in specific contexts and telling stories about them are integrated and co-dependent constituents in a narrative approach towards coaching (Stelter, 2013). Fundamentally, changing dialogues through individualised narrative coaching helps the coachee create new and alternative stories that have significance and value for the coachee and presents the context of the story from a new angle, thus encouraging different behaviours. Parkin (2003, p. 7) says that 'storytelling has always been an essential and universal human characteristic' and has three functions: to pass on information, to educate and to inspire. Stories facilitate learning and memory, as they show situations or information in the bigger picture or context. They are immersing, interesting and involve emotions and engagement. The result is that narratives give an opportunity to gain in-depth knowledge and understanding both in individual or organisational contexts (Kostera, 2008). Stories can both express identity and are tools for (re)building identity (Drake, 2018).

Storytelling as a coaching tool can be used both ways, as coachees' and coaches' narratives (Parkin, 2003), as a tool of sense-making (du Toit, 2014). For example, using a short story to establish how a coachee felt when being upset, including emotions. The coachee described this feeling in a metaphor of an erupting volcano. Discussion about the situation helped us not only to acknowledge the emotions but also to reframe the metaphor into a positive and calming visualisation: the volcano might be erupting, but it is now a volcano in Hawaii with its foot immersed in a cool ocean. Another example is the life-grid narrative interviews (Rowland et al., 2019) used as a way of getting to know the coachee at the first session and understand various influences on their life and decisions. We have found this approach particularly useful with mature coachees who wish to further their careers and with professional women to further their understanding of the impact of gender on their own (and others') behaviours.

Coachee's stories can give insight into (sometimes negative) patterns of thinking and allow for reflection on the experience or even tell the story from a different perspective. In stories, coachee's provide rich experiences which are key to how they interpret the world, and a coach can help them to identify and make desired changes (Drake, 2018). Coachee's stories, on the other hand, can be inspired by many sources, not necessarily their own experience but also mythology or popular culture – for example, gender stereotypes, and help goal setting, reframing a situation or building self-esteem (Parkin, 2003). In Appendix 1, we include five narratives taken from the study participants and accompanied them with reflective questions that can be used to interrogate these stories. We hope the stories can be of use in a group or individual coaching setting to make sense of various situations related to gender dynamics in the workplace and thus inspire change.

5.5 Metaphor

As coaches, we often face the difficulty of understanding how our coachees perceive and interpret situations. This presents a challenge as there is no direct or obvious way to access a coachee's subconsciousness. However, as coachees' use of metaphor potentially originates from their unconscious sense-making framework, metaphor offers a possible route to address the challenge. Many authors use metaphor to describe the nature of the coaching relationship, which in essence is being a 'critical friend' to discuss and explore ideas in a safe space (Passmore, 2010).

According to Parkin (2010), learning and memory can be enhanced when information is presented in a novel, out-of-the-ordinary way that does not fit with established patterns and templates in our brains. When any information does not fit into an existing and recognisable pattern, it is immediately catalogued by the neocortex as different, and the natural stress levels are raised and all sorts of alarm bells start ringing (McGaugh et al., 1990). Metaphors are one way of how we 'understand and experience one kind of thing in terms of another' (Lakoff and Johnson, 1980). They describe the way in which something is similar or different to something else, and we have found them to be very powerful in coaching. In short, metaphors carry a great deal of abstract and intangible information in a concise and memorable package.

A metaphor can be anything from a word to a short phrase, for example, 'a light at the end of a tunnel', 'stuck in a rut'. It can be used to describe how an individual sees a situation. Everyone has their own unique perspective of life, and even the same situation can be seen in different ways by different people. As such, metaphors can bring an insight into how a person has perceived a situation or event in her own life, and goals can help to capture and structure an experience. In other words, a metaphor is a comparison between two sometimes completely unrelated topics, and it is this very difference that can create a tension or a disconnect in our minds that requires resolution (Parkin, 2010). We have found that metaphors create images in the individual coachee's mind that tap into their creativity and unlock potential they may not know they have. Metaphors thus often bypass the more analytic thinking mind and directly bring aspects of life less consciously understood.

For a metaphor to work best, there has to be just enough distance between the two subjects (known as 'the topic' and 'the vehicle') for the listener to be able to make some connection but not so close as to appear overly obvious or too far away as to appear obtuse. The colourful imagery of metaphor is what helps us to remember the information and expand our learning potential – reaching beneath the surface of our experience to find a deeper truth or message that may be hidden or somewhat submerged. This brings about a deeper, insightful understanding of ourselves and others.

We find that coachee's tend to use metaphor consciously or unconsciously particularly when they feel some emotion, excitement, anger or happiness about the topic they are speaking about, which is what brings the story to life. The imagery and metaphors that any coachee uses is a rich source of data and provides information about their perception of the current reality or context. As coaches, we use metaphors to help the coachee view the situation from a completely different perspective which, in turn, breaks them out of their current situation and helps them find a solution. The coachee can consciously focus on the situation with imagination using a story, symbol or object to change their viewpoint. It can also help activate their processes of thinking, making new links in their mind and discovering something new about the situation.

In our coaching practice, we use metaphors often and have a list of metaphors to use whenever required to change a coachee's perspective about a situation. It can make the difference between being 'stuck in a rut' and being 'set free from the chains'. The use of metaphor seeks a new way of looking at things and often creates a unique turn in the coaching conversation allowing different outcomes to emerge.

Further, we have found that working with metaphors can create a sense of creativity and playfulness and help clients to see some humour in a difficult situation. The metaphor becomes memorable as we saw in our research, and the learning often has a lasting effect as the image remains accessible as in the metaphor of a mountain representing confidence in our research.

For coaches, metaphor appears to offer a route to materially enhance their understanding of a coachee's thinking offering insights into their character and values. It potentially accesses the coachee's unconscious sense-making processes and offers clear insight into how they perceive and interpret experiences. We have also found that metaphor offers significant potential for reflecting and learning from experiences and exploring one's identity, offering a potential and practical route to access insight about the unconscious sense-making processes of others.

5.6 Mindfulness and Sensory Engagement

Mindfulness is an existential approach embedding the here and now, grounding in present experience and allowing us to reconnect with the world of senses and away from unhelpful thoughts. On the one hand, mindfulness has its roots in Buddhist meditation, and on the other hand, it sources its techniques from neuroscience, a study of the brain, its functions and how various parts of our brain react to situations. It assists in rewiring our brains and connecting what we feel, think and understand (Azmatullah, 2013). Studies show that mindfulness is associated with a range of beneficial outcomes such as increased well-being, enhanced mental and physical health, behavioural and emotional regulation and greater relationship satisfaction (Cavanagh and Spence, 2013).

In a coaching context, mindfulness has been used to reduce stress, anxiety, enhance work–life balance, build resilience, focus on happiness and deal with uncertainty and change, as well as leadership development (Hall, 2015). In fact, mindfulness has been embedded in some of the key leadership models such as Scharmer's Theory U (2007) and authentic leadership (Lee and Roberts, 2010). Theory U states that in order to liberate oneself from unhelpful past patterns of behaviour, one needs to engage with 'presenting': sensing + presence (Scharmer, 2007). Meanwhile, authentic leadership theory emphasises the necessity of exploring 'true self' through adopting a reflective stance (Lee and Roberts, 2010). In our workshops (Chapter 4), mindfulness was used extensively in Workshop One in the form of guided meditations, relaxation exercises and sensory engagement.

We have positive personal experiences with mindfulness exercises and see its value in allowing a coachee to properly check-in to the session, focus on the key themes and to regulate emotional responses. There is a plenitude of mindfulness exercises that can be used during coaching sessions: breathing, body sensation, focussing on external sounds and 'thoughts acknowledging' (Annasley et al., 2015). Each of these aims to bring consciousness to the present, turning off the autopilot and focussing on the links between feelings, sensations and impulses (Chaskalson & McMordie, 2018). Mindfulness can help to notice and explore sensations, and this sensory engagement roots us in the present moment. We define sensory engagement here as engaging with our senses to get involved emotionally and foster a sense of connectedness. The body scan is one of the key but simple tools used in mindfulness-based therapies and can be easily adapted for a coaching session. You can ask the coachee to sit comfortably, close their eyes and move their attention to body parts, noticing sensations in the feet, legs, stomach, arms and head. There are a couple of common outcomes of this exercise. Firstly, people tend to notice that their mind is wandering away and they need to remind themselves where the focus is. Second, people acknowledge sensations that they have not noticed before and the discovery can be revealing. Third, some people find it relaxing to the extent they want to fall asleep, and some feel the tension, the need to go back to the normal mode of (over) thinking. Either way, these are the first steps of becoming more conscientious, focussed and happy.

In our own coaching practice, we have used breathing and grounding exercises as a way of cutting off distractions and a sense of urgency. The exercise we have found the most challenging was trying not to think about anything but the present moment, and if any thoughts would appear, we dismiss them by classifying them as either 'past' or 'future'. We have also used 'coaching whilst walking', which combines exercise and contact with nature to ground in conversation (Homer, 2019). We consider the natural environment and surroundings as a helper with bringing mind to presence: listening to the birds, feeling the warmth of sunshine on one's face, noticing the humid air or rain on one's skin and adjusting breath to the pace of walk (it's worth trying!).

Finally, it is worth mentioning that mindfulness might not be for everyone. Some people have spiritual connotations with mindfulness meditation or are not ready to engage with the daily practice necessary for the approach to work (Hall, 2015). Moreover, mindfulness has recently been criticised for internalising problems that may have external sources (Purser, 2019). As coaches, we need to remember that any tool we use is to enable and let flourish, by recognising both internal and external barriers and overcoming them.

5.7 Concluding Reflections

Our critical position has been to place the women's voices, perspectives and real-life gender stereotype threat situations at the heart of our work (grounded accounts), as much research has focussed on a more scientific approach involving 'priming' or 'non-priming' of women (a technique whereby exposure to one stimulus influences a response to a subsequent stimulus, without conscious guidance or intention, rather than be set in a 'real-life' situation). We argue that placing professional women's experiences at the centre of our work has been valuable and enabled a fuller explanation of the topic and has contributed to elaborate on the conditions that one should encourage and avoid.

It is clear that subtle and inevitable forms of gender stereotypic behaviours are hampering professional women's progress by obstructing their identity, thereby perpetuating these gender stereotypes in the workplace. This evaluation demands a new approach through individual or group coaching for women. Only by designing arts-based coaching for women that meets their needs, and addresses the gendered issues identified by women themselves, can we really support their careers. This approach will give professional women an opportunity to interact with other women who are solely fit to give the support, corroboration, and the social consideration they need. This is not about teaching women the rules of the game established by men, rather to recognise social context and 'self' to better prepare women for leadership.

We boldly suggest that a new theory of incorporating arts-based methods through a positive psychology coaching approach, that can be individualised or collaborative, focussed on an issue owned by an individual or a group, will moderate gender stereotype threat. The approach needs to allow individuals to focus on a personal and specific gender issue through being placed in the gender stereotype threatening domain and engaging in 'sensory and metaphorical experience'. Using arts-based methods in coaching offers a 'complementary' approach to current professional development by demonstrating that less rational-orientated experiential learning methods provide a constructive platform to explore gender, allowing individuals to have access to 'unconscious' gendered behaviours by questioning notions of social realities to challenge the complexities of gender and create specific action and opportunity in a gendered work environment. This is extremely important as individuals are increasingly likely to identify strongly with multiple groups simultaneously and feel social identity conflict, given the complexity of the social world.

In summary, many coaches have experienced working with arts and creativity in their practice and have also experienced the insightful and transformative outcomes that come from working this way. We feel that the art in coaching is under-rated, perhaps because of our own perceptions and assumptions of arts and our own creative abilities. In reality, coaching with arts is a very powerful tool that deepens awareness and understanding in a way that shifts perceptions and leads to transformational change.

We make bold claims about the potential of arts-based methods in coaching to bring about a change in the way that gender stereotype threat is perceived by professional women and others. In doing so, we are not suggesting a replacement of more conventional professional development practices, rather that coaching will provide a valuable addition to the current dominant pedagogy. The hope is to influence gender stereotype threats that can be moderated or eliminated and to create circumstances that do not judge women, before they have a chance to act. We are hopeful that this book and the subsequent knowledge-sharing activities will stimulate further analysis, consideration and discussion of its findings.

Finally, we are critically aware of the significant danger of individualising the impact of gender stereotype threat if this had been the only focus of our work, but this was not our intention. We believe that organisations and societies need to reconsider their current equality approaches and incorporate support for the individuals in addition to investing in systemic change. It is clear that for professional women to advance their careers in their organisational worlds, identity becomes critically important as, essentially, women's sense of self is being challenged to enable 'fit' in their masculine worlds. I share Samantha's reflections that echo the sentiments of many women in this study, as she described her career journey to date in the shadow of gender stereotype threat:

> *It's been like fighting through black fog, whilst walking on marshmallow. not really knowing where I'm going, it's never been clear, I've never been really true to myself. I pull back all of the time, because I'm frightened of judgement.*

The ability to reflect on women's current circumstances both in society and the workplace can specifically help us, women, to rethink our 'given' place and reshape the world around us.

5.8 The Future

Who knows, the Covid-19 pandemic could be a catalyst in progressing women's equality in the workplace, but arguably, it has slowed the progress further. It is imperative that research continues in this area if women are to gain great access to leadership positions. The findings of our work could be enhanced further by exploring (i) specific threats identified in childhood that continue to impact women's careers (for example, a strong male culture or impact of toxic masculinity); (ii) what other types of arts-based coaching techniques could moderate gender stereotype threat; (iii) the potential to standardise the arts-based

coaching approach by focussing on a specific perceived gender stereotype threat; (iv) the sustainability of the learning outcomes over a longer
time period; (v) specific arts-based coaching as part of an organisational
cultural change process aimed at gendered issues in the workplace; (vi)
the broader representation of participants, specifically those outside
of the North East of England and (vii) the extent to which arts-based
coaching could support men in exploring gender stereotype threat and
gendered behaviours in the workplace.

*Gender Bias in Organisations: From the Arts to Individualised
Coaching* is a book to shift thinking and open up new possibilities, to
stimulate fresh insight and to adapt the creativity and learning from
arts-based workshops to an arts-based approach in coaching and
mentoring in practice. This book will be an invaluable companion for
learning and development professionals and those working in Human
Resource departments in addition to individuals who wish to self-
develop, coaches and mentors, coaching and mentoring students and
trainees, and coach supervisors.

Appendix 1: Case Studies

A.1 Jennifer's Story

A.1.1 Overview

Jennifer had agreed to meet with me as a 'professional friend'. She had been clear that she would not take part in the study herself but had been willing to listen to the interviewer's ideas. Towards the end of our discussion, she described how the 'hairs stood up on the back of her neck'. She had no explanation for this feeling; she just knew that she had to participate.

Jennifer had been a successful business owner for many years and described herself as someone with 'a lot of internal confidence'. Her inner confidence had, however, never quite matched other people's high regard for her. Jennifer had been very successful in her career but was seeking to hand over the business to her partner. She was ready 'to do something for herself'.

What is of particular interest in her story is her portrayal of the evaporation of self-belief co-existing with internal confidence and the profound impact the arts-based workshop has had on her self-belief and future career.

A.1.2 Career History

Jennifer had initially attended an all-girls school in the South of England and then at 15 years of age had transferred to a comprehensive mixed school in the North East of England. She had never flourished academically there. As she prepared to leave school at 16, she could not remember anybody guiding her. Her parents had not been to university but had encouraged her to have a career. Jennifer had recognised her creative ability and was keen to go straight into employment. She got a job as a window dresser in a major high street store. A year later, she decided to return to college for one year to complete her schooling.

Her mother was a sound role model for career women, having worked all her life, initially in distribution and later in journalism. She identified an opportunity for Jennifer as a receptionist in a creative service, which Jennifer had embraced. Later, the manager approached Jennifer with a business idea and told her about a trainee position, which had a non-graduate route. This position was the opportunity Jennifer needed, and she joined the new business which was a significant career move for Jennifer. She progressed well in this industry, as it provided a conducive climate, she had a natural flair and her talents were appreciated, '*I didn't understand the theory of it, I could do it, ... I was a natural*'.

Jennifer had worked in this business 17 years before setting up on her own. A business she had expanded over time. Jennifer spoke with special pride about what she had achieved, business awards, strong professional networks, a financially strong business and a business partner. She also outlined her beliefs about her 'grandmother' role of supporting her team, taking an interest in their lives and celebrating their successes. Despite her obvious business success, and her 'great career', Jennifer described how she was losing passion for this type of work, and was ready 'to do something for herself'.

A.1.3 New Opportunities

Jennifer was 'headhunted' to chair a prestigious community development board in the town in which one of her businesses was located. In her career to date, she had always believed that her appearance, southern accent and humour had opened doors for her and did her no harm in an environment where people were very conscious of fashion and looking good, but the conflict in Jennifer's image was her perceived lack of education. As the stereotype threat was aroused, the evaporation of self-belief was apparent, '*I ain't got the skills to do this, I haven't got the vocabulary, ... I don't know how to chair a meeting*'. Over a few months, Jennifer had received constructive support from her peer group who believed her to be the right person for the job, 'the front man'. Jennifer finally accepted the position.

Board members were primarily men and seemed to be focussed on key performance indicators (KPIs) and marketing. She found that some of the men did not take responsibility for their actions to make the venture a success, and she felt that this made her role more difficult, '*I would study it* [the board reports], *I would have the numbers, I would have it like that'*. This perceived lack of co-operation made her angry, but she judged her own aggression as the opposite of being vulnerable, anxious, rational, reasonable, listening. She wrote a poem during the workshop that expressed the sensory experience:

> The time I feel vulnerable
> The time I feel anxious
> Be careful it can be perishable
> It's time to get comfortable
>
> You truly are precious
> The others are dangerous
>
> How can you become calm?
> Careful not to harm
> You are not in a prison
> Don't hasten, just listen
>
> No need to rush
> Clean out with a new brush
> What's the dash?
> Stop you will crash
>
> Think comfortable, think precious
> You don't always need to win
> It's brilliant just to finish

She took several photographs that expressed her sensory experience (for example, listening, racing against time, feeling vulnerable, constantly running and a sense of clutter in her head).

Jennifer explored the sensory experience of the problem through words relating to sensation and through sharing her photographs with other workshop participants. In this exploration, she did not only focus on the sensory experience of the problem, but it was also clear she was looking for a way forward in both the sensory words and photographs, for example, reflecting on experiences of life, recognising that feeling vulnerable is dangerous, how precious we are, comfortable and calm.

In her post-workshop interview, Jennifer described a recent board meeting. She experienced the meeting differently. She had felt more confident and had not spent as much time preparing. She believed the reason for this new behaviour was the discussion in the workshop about using the metaphor of a mountain for self-confidence, '*I've got the knowledge. I am a mountain*'. Jennifer had thought about the 'solidness' of the mountain many times since the workshop and had shared the metaphor with others. She shared the story of a difficult board meeting discussion in which she felt that board members had put 'a bomb' on her mountain. She described her sense of calmness in the situation which she would 'have taken personally' in the past. She summed up the behavioural changes after the arts-based intervention as:

> *understanding the word confidence, and the fact and meaning realisation that confidence is a fact, it's not an emotion ... [it's about] not letting people chip at it, or rain on it, or snow on it. It can do that, but the centre of that mountain is solid and holding onto that, you are who you are, and celebrate that dawn.*

Jennifer had a new understanding of confidence that has had a profound effect on her. She described feeling a sense of solidness, a new feeling for her. She is confident that the feeling is sustainable, '*you can't remember the words, but I can always remember a happy time ... it resonated with me ... and that's something I can carry around*'.

A.1.4 Reflection

This story can be used to discuss issues such as influencing, assertiveness, self-esteem and personal achievement.

1. What is your inner voice saying? Is this healthy and helpful?
2. How could you make the inner voice more helpful to your future?
3. Do you cherish yourself as well as others?
4. In what ways do you demonstrate that you cherish yourself?
5. How do you feel about cherishing yourself – guilty?
6. Assertiveness is about finding a balance between your own needs and those of others. Do you achieve this balance?

A.2 Samantha's Story

> *I've a huge personality, but it's almost like I restrain it, I pull back all of the time because I'm frightened of judgement, even more so when I'm in a male-dominated environment. I feel I'm always about to pop a cork, but don't quite get there, because I'm frightened of what the fizz will do. So I'm just pulling back all of the time.*

A.2.1 Overview

Samantha volunteered to participate in the research having been told about it by a friend. She had worked in a heavily male-dominated organisational environment and culture in another country and felt that her experience would benefit the study. She found women in that environment to be confrontational and unsupportive, and the men subjected her to personalised sexual behaviours.

She felt angry about the vulnerability she felt in that hostile environment, and in her own behaviours of replacing feminine traits with masculine traits, '*they would see this strong character, but as soon as I got home I would crumble*'.

This experience was difficult for Samantha, '*I had to delve deeper than I'd ever delved before for inner strength*'. Eventually, the situation became too hard for her to bear, and she 'exploded' in the office. This was a turning point for Samantha. Following the 'incident', she felt more respect from her colleagues and in time recognised that the experience had given her strength and determination.

Three years ago, in her late thirties, Samantha had her first baby, which she described as the most exciting and motivating time in her life. She had recently set up her own business, an adventure she is finding challenging but enjoyable.

A.2.2 A Difficult Early Career

Samantha's early career was not planned. She was lacking in self-confidence and unclear of her options. Her first role was as an export manager and is the main focus of her involvement in the research. Her subsequent roles were in the UK, where she held a wide range of positions. Initially as a marketing assistant, a role in which she felt very comfortable, and in which she grew in self-confidence. Unfortunately, this situation was short lived when she was made redundant.

Feeling very discouraged, Samantha made a 'knee jerk' decision to travel, '*I thought right that's it, I'm going to be a "trolley dolly"*', a position she felt met with others' expectations of women and her feeling of 'worthlessness'. Samantha successfully completed her training and became 'a waitress in the sky'. Then disaster stuck, '*I only lasted two flights as September 11th happened, and I was made redundant again*'. Samantha was to be made redundant twice more before her career started to settle down, '*it's been like fighting through black fog, whilst walking on marshmallow*'.

A.2.3 Doubt and Isolation

Samantha had been the first woman in the position of export manager. Her first months in her organisation were confusing and shocking, as she realised that the women working there were in administrative roles, and she was the only woman manager. Samantha soon learned that her professional expertise was not welcomed in the organisation: *'they didn't support me'*, *'they feared me'*. She believed that this attitude was because of the different culture. During her time in this role, Samantha felt she had no choice but to focus on her work. She felt extremely lonely and isolated, as she tried to balance her behaviours in this challenging environment, *'I'm like a contradiction, I'm hard and I'm soft both at the same time'*.

Samantha found that personalised sexual behaviours were commonplace in this environment. She described feeling comfortable during the day but exposed in her evening work with 'sexually charged males', who were invariably drinking alcohol, *'I felt very vulnerable in these one-to-one situations ... from a sexual perspective'*. Later, she learned that people believed she must have been sleeping with the export director to get her management position.

Samantha was also out of place as a woman in that culture. She was surprised that the women did not speak to her for nine months. Around her, they would start whispering as she walked by and comment on how she dressed *'they called me Margaret Thatcher because I dressed with a tie'*.

Samantha finally felt a level of anger and despair that she could not contain and exploded in the office. She described the situation as blood rushing to her head, her arms and hands were tingling, and she shouted very loudly *'what is wrong with you people'*. She recalls seeing the shock on their faces. A reaction that she feels was their acknowledgement of 'overstepping the mark'. As time passed, Samantha recognised that she had gained strength and determination from the experience and an element of respect from her colleagues.

A.2.4 Removing Negative Judgements of Self

Samantha's experience of the arts-based workshop was positive. She felt it had given her [and others] 'room to breathe' and share their vulnerability, *'it was like an invisible connection between us all, like unspoken, but felt'*.

Samantha returned to her first role in sharing her 'problem' with the group. She described not feeling natural, as she replaces feminine traits with masculine traits, '*I have a huge personality, but I restrain it*'. A situation that angers her. She wrote a poem to express the sensory experience of her anger and control of her feelings:

> *Your words are troubling, you have my mind bubbling,*
> *I need to stop this worrying, before this situation has me boiling,*
> *So I make myself steady, make sure that I am ready,*
> *But why do I feel so heavy?*
> *As I try to control my feelings, I cannot stop my mind buzzing,*
> *My fingers are tingling, as I look at the ceiling to try and centre my*
>   *feelings,*
> *I do not want to hide the feeling, I want to have freedom,*
> *I want to feel wholesome, and no longer lonesome.*

She took a number of photographs to express her sensory experience, but one photograph made a particular impression on her, as it was the only photograph she remembered post-interview. It was stone boulders.

This came to represent the experience of women shedding their personality to become uniformed and adapt to what is expected of them, '*we are all in a row and we have to do what we are told*'. This perspective was not new for her.

Image 8 Stone boulders (Case Study 2, Appendix 1)

Shortly after the workshop, Samantha had an encounter with male colleagues that placed her in a situation where she would have previously conformed to. However, she experienced that encounter differently, *'there were some younger men in there [the meeting], and they crossed the line in the things they were saying, untoward things. The old me would have taken it to heart, or got angry with them. I said ... "you can carry on if you like, but it's not going to have any affect on me. So, if you want to talk amongst yourselves, then do so, but you're wasting your energy"'*.

Her perception of the situation was changing and was visible in the strength of her words and actions. She described how she had been able to tackle the situation 'head on', *'the old me would have taken it to heart'*, *'... has it affected me, no'*. Samantha confirmed that on her drive home from the workshop she had felt uplifted and engaged with herself again. She had realised that her experiences were more common than she had believed, *'you start thinking it is something personal, and it's not, it's your gender. It's not you as an individual'*.

A.2.5 Reflection

You might use this story to discuss issues such as seeing a situation from a different perspective and differentiating what could be changed to what cannot be changed.

1. What do you restrain in your life? How could you unleash that?
2. Have you or someone you know displayed masculine traits? What was the situation?
3. Have you ever 'exploded' at work? Could you have had a different response to the situation? What would you need to do to enact a different response?
4. What represents the 'stone boulders' in your life or at work? What cannot be changed, what could be changed?
5. When have you felt 'room to breathe'? What could you do to keep this feeling?
6. In what situation are you, or someone you know feeling the impact of your gender? How could you change this?

A.3 Linda's Story

A.3.1 Overview

Linda agreed to participate in the research, having heard about it through a work colleague. She was very enthusiastic about her role as gender equality lead in her organisation, which she performs in addition to her full-time job. Her vision of diversifying the organisation in the future was clear. She felt that her male-dominated sector was 'shocking' in this day and age, with 95% of employees being men, and this research would be a useful reference point for the equality group she chairs. She had been with her male-dominated organisation for 14 years, in a culture that was not always sympathetic to gender equality. Some senior managers were confrontational and abusive to each other and had at times adopted the same style towards Linda. She developed various strategies for coping in this hostile environment, becoming tougher and aggressive when it was needed. Her working life was a continual fight. More recently, she has placed her faith in a new 'Chief', who she believes will be a champion for gender equality. Her account offers insight to working in a male-dominated environment, which had significant gender relational challenges and subsequent impact.

A.3.2 Background

Linda is a single woman in her late thirties with no children. She went to university when she was in her early twenties which she described as a 'brilliant experience'. She had not planned to join a public service, '*it was just one of those things*'. Her initial role got her interested in the service, which was timely, as she was '*still trying to figure out what to do when she was grown up*'. At the end of an initial contract, with a lot of support and encouragement from a male colleague, she applied for a permanent job. A few years later, he also mentored and coached her for promotion, and she became the first person to move from a non-uniformed position to a uniformed position, '*it was a really positive thing as it opened a lot of different opportunities*'. She was the only woman in that rank and a corporate member of staff.

Linda felt that she was given the opportunity because she was a 'breath of fresh air' and was committed to make a difference to help the organisation diversify. Not everyone was supportive of Linda's appointment, some [men] felt she was taking a job away from them, '*you're going to get the job because you're a woman, they need to tick the box*'. This last move had so much promise but turned into a disappointment due to 'ranking' blockages created by recruitment policies and processes, '*I've been doing this job for 9 years, and now there is nowhere for me to go*'.

A.3.3 Experiences in a Male-dominated Culture

Linda has assessed her organisations culture and discovered a level of acceptance of the environment, '*I can't tell you how many women I've heard say I just want to fit in with the lads'*, and when she reported a senior manager for 'unacceptable' behaviour, she was advised by the Human Resources team to, *'just go off on the sick'*. Managers deal with each other, and other staff aggressively, using blunt, confronting language, *'you are up and down like a tap dancer's wig. He meant I'm not resilient'*. In the early part of her career, Linda had started to feel prescriptive gender stereotype threats from several perspectives. Firstly, being viewed as a woman as a result of career progression expectations, *'you have to be seen to stand toe to toe with a man, and win that "shouty" argument, so they don't see you as a little girl'*. Secondly, she was expected to behave like a woman by being obedient and respectful, and she saw others being treated in this way, *'he would constantly give people very tight deadlines … he would demand to know why it hadn't been done in front of colleagues and consultants'*.

Linda, as the only woman at her management level, recognises the powerful bond of the men, *'every time somebody retires or there is a significant birthday, they will go on a day trip … they leave at 8.30am, drink on the train, then drink in the pubs, … there has even been discussion of a strip club in the past. Not something I would do'*.

A.3.4 Starting to Question

An array of factors began to contribute to the questioning that eventually led Linda to consider seeking a new role outside of this environment. Linda was feeling a descriptive stereotype threat to her proven competence and ambition. The questioning was partly prompted by the blockages in promotion opportunities, *'I'm just going to go somewhere new where I can see there's a career path'*. She was also feeling the cost of acting 'out of character', *'I'm not averse to making my presence felt, but I'm disappointed if I have to get to that stage'*. Linda felt her value base was being challenged as she was continually 'wheeled out' as the women in uniform for every assessment and audit, *'it was look we've got a woman, and now ten years later I'm still the only woman … oh yes, let's tick the box'*. She also questioned the value of the many awards and accreditations the organisation had acquired, *'it looks great on paper, but it makes very little difference'*.

Later, Linda emphasised her continuing faith in the kind of culture her organisation was striving to develop, *'I've gone through the whole change curve of fury, to upset, to anger to I'm just going to get another job to no, I'm going to fight this, and I'm going to be the one that breaks through for other people'*.

A.3.5 Increased Self-reflection and Removal of Negative Judgement of Others

In her post-workshop interview, Linda directly expressed that she no longer believed in the negative judgement of self and others, which she had expressed prior to the arts intervention. In her narrative, she described alternatives, which she believed would explain others' behaviour.

In her pre-workshop interview, Linda had described a strained relationship with her line manager, who she felt was blocking her career progression. Her line manager was being told what to do by a senior male officer, and she had obeyed, as expected, in this type of environment, '*I was disappointed at her for not standing up for me as a woman, and standing up for me as one of her direct reports ... I was quite frustrated with her ... I was really upset, I went home and cried*'.

Linda had perceived a lack of fit between her line manager's actions and the equality values of the organisation. She had felt a complete lack of support from her line manager, something that Linda would not do to her own staff. She had felt she could 'fight the good fight', be strong and 'stand up', but sometimes she got tired of being the one, '*it would be nice to have an easy life*'.

In her post-workshop interview, Linda had changed the way she perceived and engaged with a situation described pre-workshop. She recognised her own behaviours of '*getting increasingly frustrated with her line manager*'. She told a story about reflecting on her own behaviour, '*I was so hacked off, I wonder if that's reflected how I'm behaving at work ... how I am with others*'. She saw that the behaviour displayed by her line manager was not in her character, prompting Linda to reconsider how the major organisational change agenda may be affecting her line manager. She concluded that, '*she may be in a worse place than me*'. Linda saw this as new behaviour for her, '*I feel better equipped*', [to deal with this situation].

Through the performance of the story As You Like It, Linda had become aware of the many characters in the play which she could align to the players in her organisation, '*even some of the trickier characters in the play ... you could see where they were coming from*'. She specifically recalled a woman [Rosalind] who in the play dressed as a man to be safe and accepted. This had resonated with Linda and how she feels in her male-dominated environment. She described sometimes having to be authoritarian, but also could sometimes be completely herself, with a range of emotions in between, '*the best way to describe it is it's a mess*'. Linda had felt physically worn out prior to the workshop; however, post-workshop she had felt, '*it was time to regenerate, and to think about your behaviour towards others*'.

A.3.6 Reflection

This story can be used to explore organisational culture, independent and creative thought, valuing the power of experience and personal empowerment.

1. Do the rules in your organisation help or hinder creativity and empowerment?
2. Are there some procedures that need revising?
3. How do people learn in your organisation?
4. How is experience valued?
5. What stops you, or others, from changing?
6. How could you encourage more innovation?

A.4 Kayley's Story

A.4.1 Overview

Kayley left school at 15 years of age with '*no personal expectations of her career path*'. She spent her early career working in a factory, which she felt met the expectations for women in her home area. In her early twenties, she decided to explore other options, moving away from home to take up various positions, which she felt had given her independence and experience. After two years away from home, she became disillusioned with the cost of living in the South of England, so moved back to the North – Liverpool. The company she joined offered her an opportunity to move into Human Resource Management (HRM), where she grew with it before making her move to a large corporate organisation. In her early forties, she began questioning her lifestyle, and with her children being just seven and nine decided that she would like more flexibility in caring decisions and became self-employed, running her own human resource consultancy business. Initially, the business was very successful, but when the North was hit by recession, she found it difficult to get work. This, coupled with her husband being made redundant, resulted in the business folding. Despite feeling '*a bit of a failure*'. Kayley is hugely proud of her success as an entrepreneur, describing her gain as '*personal and emotional resilience, and increased self-confidence*'. Kayley has continued to grow her career in personnel management and organisational development but feels she has probably plateaued in her current not-for-profit organisation, confirming that her career aspirations are on hold until her two children go to university.

A.4.2 Early Career History

Kayley was the last of four children and by the time it came to the fourth time around her parents often did not go to school parents evening, they had *'no expectations of me'*. Upon her return to the North, Kayley met a female role model whom she described as personally driven, but who also pushed her *'she really did challenge me, and I enjoyed the challenge'*. She had recognised Kayley's ability, flexibility and hard work and 'shoe-horned' her into a role in human resources, prompting Kayley to start thinking about a career. She returned to education in pursuit of a career, initially to upgrade her GCSE results and then in her late twenties, she went on to gain a Certificate in Personnel Practice, returning to education again in her late thirties to upgrade her qualification to a master's level, a qualification of which she is immensely proud. Over those years, she continued to grow in her field, gaining a breadth of valuable experience, building her social networks along the way particularly while working in a large prestigious organisation, a career tactic she has sustained as it *'gives her oxygen'*.

A.4.3 An Opportunity to Prove Herself

Kayley grew up in a typically gendered environment. She describes her home environment as *'the women did the cooking or tidying up, and the men were in a huddle somewhere probably drinking'* and her school environment as *'the boys got to carry the milk crates, whilst the girls got to give out the straws'*. Kayley grew up with a need to compete. She was aware of people's low expectations of women and describes her diversity management experiences as *'ticking boxes'* and more recent diversity efforts in her current organisation as interesting but restricted to a management level, rather than involving all staff. Quality and fairness are really important to Kayley: *'I've always been interested in stories about women's rights, you know "Made in Dagenham". I showed it to my children'*. She describes an early childhood memory as having to *'scrabble and fight for her place around the table, to be heard, to be listened too, and to be considered … I was dismissed quite a lot'*. She felt angry at her brothers for being tough with her at the tender age of four or five:

> *I had a little yellow bear called Barnaby, and they played piggy in the middle with it. Every time they got it they punched it, threw it across*

me, and then did the same again ... it was tough, I just wanted to cry and I did. This is one of my early memories.

A.4.4 Macho Management and Post-heroic Leadership Traits

What is of particular interest in her interview transcript is the extent to which she discusses the co-existence of macho-management and post-heroic leadership traits. Kayley had clear ideas about what portrays effective leadership including resilience, trust, risk-taker, action orientated, future focussed, honest, open and transparent. Kayley's narrative presents her as a people person, a team player. She described making a deliberate shift away from adopting her typically feminine approach, towards the adoption of a masculine subject position. She presented a more competitive and driven approach when faced with an aroused gender stereotype threat. '*I need to be dominant, when taking on a man in the workplace. I don't want to walk into a room, and let a man think that they are messing on me*'. Her transcripts have many examples of ways in which she learned to think like a man in some aspects of her work. She also confirms that this is not who she wants to be, '*I want to be calm, thoughtful, and considered*'.

A.4.5 Hiding Behind the Sword

When I met Kayley post-workshop, she was enthusiastic about the workshop facilitator and the programme. The experience was an important source of learning for Kayley as she linked aspects of the 'artful' story to her organisation's 'performance' culture, – '*you need resilience to work here*'.

The most striking revelation in this story was when she described her key observation from the As You Like It performance as needing to show vulnerability to be resilient, '*I think the first thing you think about is you've got to be tough, hard and mean, but I don't think that's the case at all*'. She realised that when she is feeling vulnerable, she has a tendency to use her human resources knowledge to construct herself as a powerful force in the workplace, '*it's just like a can opener ... not what I want to use it for really, just to get in*'. She reflected that organisational development is a big part of her job, '*it's cultural and that's difficult. I want them to think she knows her onions here ... let's hear what she has to say*'.

Kayley was given an opportunity in the workshop to 'lay down the sword', to stop using her profession as a 'crutch' and perhaps show her vulnerability, but she chose not to do so. In her post-workshop interview, she justified this action: '*I probably would only use the sword to get around the table to then influence. I really want to influence people*'.

It is apparent from the transcripts that Kayley's not-for-profit organisation was undergoing a significant change and places a premium value on achieving targets to secure funds for future service delivery, thereby reinforcing male values. We conclude that Kayley chooses to use this approach as one of many subject positions to construct herself as a powerful force in dealing with gender stereotype threat.

A.4.6 *Reflection*

You can use this story to help people to see their beliefs from a different perspective.

1. Have you been influenced by other people? In what way?
2. Are your beliefs holding you back in some way?
3. Are there any beliefs you might want to change? How could you change them?
4. What effect would this change have on your life?
5. Have you adopted a masculine subject position as a woman or a feminine subject position as a man? What were the circumstances that led to this stance?
6. How resilient do you feel? How could you increase your resilience (ability to recover quickly from difficult situations)?

A.5 Justine's Story

A.5.1 *Overview*

Justine was in her mid-fifties when we met and leading a relatively new team within a joint structure of health and social care professionals. The relationship with her male line manager was becoming increasingly difficult, a situation that was engulfing Justine and which became the focus of her involvement in this study. She was feeling a prescriptive stereotype threat because she was displaying a concern for others and in exposing defiance to an expectation of obedience. She was also feeling a descriptive stereotype threat due to displaying independence, and decisiveness, which eventually became untenable. Her account of events offer insight into the potentially difficult power dynamics involved in organisational cultural change, which has significant gender associations.

A.5.2 Early Career

Following a period of ill-health, Justine got her first job at 21. Her role was to secure welfare rights for vulnerable people, and this task soon became a passion for Justine, forming the basis of her long career, *'it fits my personality, and politics'*. At that time, Justine had a supportive manager that she considered a role model, *'she had quite severe disabilities, but she was the least disabled person I've come across to date'*. Justine was encouraged to move forward with her innovative ideas to support a wider range of vulnerable people, gaining experience and self-confidence. She continued her social care career and achieved a Diploma in Social Work in her mid-forties. She is particularly proud of her time as a homeless resettlement officer working with 'optimistic' teenagers, whom she felt *'deserved a chance'*. Justine felt that this was a particularly 'humbling experience'.

A.5.3 Stepping into a New Challenge

Justine moved into a management role in 2013 within a newly formed integrated service of social care and health services. Justine was supportive of this change and described it as an opportunity to improve services for clients with no artificial structural barriers. Justine's new organisation had a performance culture, which she felt was becoming more and more entrenched. The focus was on achieving targets, rather than working with people, *'we don't work with tins of beans, you can't stick them on a shelf and count them, we work with people'*.

Justine started to challenge this new culture and had little respect for her male line manager, whom she described as a 'business type', rather than a social worker or a nurse, *'he's a puppet, he tows the line'*, *'he's like a rabbit in the headlights when you talk about patients'*, *'he's not a strong man, nor does he have a strong personality'*. She had started to feel prescriptive stereotype threats from two perspectives. Firstly, being viewed as a woman because she displayed kindness and was sympathetic to her profession and its professional views. Secondly, she was expected to behave as a woman by being obedient, *'everything just had to be done'*, and there was no opportunity to ask questions. The cultures were so different, *'it's like somebody says jump to a "health" person ... and they say ... how high? Ask that of a social worker, they will say jump, well can we skip a little bit'*.

At this stage, Justine had to live with three major forces, which together eventually eroded her ability to stay in her position: firstly, powerful organisational players, who felt threatened by the challenge of social work principles and reacted against them. Secondly, the power processes itself, as her line manager withdrew his support for her. Thirdly, she felt that she was unable to adequately communicate her strong professional beliefs and concern for others, and that those beliefs were being continually challenged.

A.5.4 The Situation Came to a Head

Justine saw this juncture as a critical time. The battle-lines became hardened as she displayed descriptive gender stereotypic behaviours of independence, self-reliance and decisiveness. Her position and behaviours became more visible, and the situation became untenable. Justine felt that she had let her social work team down, '*it felt like a slur on my professional integrity, which I hold very dear*'. She told the story of how she had felt during the meeting in which she was told of her fate, '*tears and anger, but frustration more than anything*'. She had felt vulnerable and thought she was being judged as a woman, '*I did feel when I came away that they are going to think I'm crying because I'm a bloody woman*'.

A.5.5 Negative Judgement of Others

Justine felt very engaged in the arts-based workshop and understood the 'artistic endeavour'. She particularly remembered the powerfulness of the photography and the poetry.

In her photographs, she used a sign displaying the words '*feed me non-recyclable waste only please*' to represent her line manager '*going over the same thing, again, and again, and again*', [her inference being the performance targets], a soft leather seat represented 'darkness and uncomfortableness'. There was also a more positive illustration of a life-belt representing a colleague coming to the rescue, and a picture of the sky, showing some light, that she described as '*wanting something bigger than me*'. Justine remembered many of her photographs in the post-workshop interview and in particular referenced the rubbish bins and a fire escape sign. They made a significant impression on her.

The picture of the rubbish bins came to represent the experience of '*varying degrees of rubbish*'. She confirmed that the colours of the bins represented her feelings, '*the hurt*' [orange] and '*the calm in her mind*' [blue]. The fire escape sign came to represent '*man taking me down, … it was a dark sort of roller coaster*', which she described as very hurtful.

Justine was one of only two women who did not experience a removal of negative judgements of others' behaviours or her own emotions. She

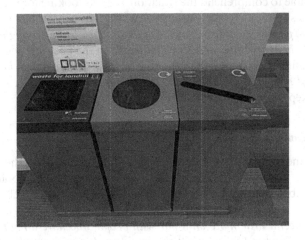

Image 9 Rubbish bins (Case Study 5, Appendix 1)

Image 10 Exit sign (Case Study 5, Appendix 1)

had strong judgements of others' behaviours, which were untouched by the process.

By the time we interviewed Justine post-workshop, she was in a different role. In the post-workshop interview, she kept seeing her ex-boss as unable to comprehend the situation and was looking for ways to explain the situation. In the pre-interview, she saw the problem in terms of, '*he's a puppet, he tows the line. He's like a rabbit in the headlights when you talk about anything to do with patients*'. In the post-interview, she kept the same metaphor of the situation, '*it's like I'm looking at him as some sort of puppet, I can almost see the strings, I can almost see the strings*', and kept her judgement of her ex-boss.

A.5.6 *Re-affirming Self-worth*

However, Justine confirmed a greater level of confidence post-workshop, describing it as the ability to ground and visualise what is solid about you. She described this using the metaphor of 'orange polished steel':

> *I actually feel a little more on a par with people who have a higher role, … that's what I mean about the confident. It's orange, polished steel, that's what I feel. That's where I am now. There is an orange brightness and that polished steel is something a little bit more refined than it was before.*

The interpretation I place on this is that the metaphors used in the workshop confirmed her pre-workshop feelings. She subsequently affirmed her self-worth, protecting herself from the perceived threat and the consequence of failure. She also recognised a need to increase self-control.

A.5.7 *Reflection*

You can use this story to explore flexible and creative thinking, taking a different vantage point and reframing an issue or problem.

1. Have you, or someone you know, been involved in organisational cultural change. Did you or they feel any sense of impact due to gender?
2. Are you too rigid in your thinking at times? In what way?
3. How could you see things differently?
4. Is there something or someone you could see in a more positive light?
5. Have you had a time when you've felt 'darkness and uncomfortableness'? How did you deal with it?
6. Do you listen to others' views with an open mind?

Appendix 2: Glossary of Key Terms

Arts-based interventions encompass working with art(s) and creativity to address a personal or workplace challenge. A wide range of art can be used including drawing, poetry, photographs/pictures, storytelling, music and theatre.

Gender stereotype threat is the fear that a person's behaviour may confirm an existing stereotype of a group with which that person identifies (Steele, 1997), which can negatively impact an individual's behaviour.

Metaphor is a comparison between two unrelated topics, for example, 'a light at the end of a tunnel'.

Mindfulness is an existential approach embedding the here and now, grounding in present experience and allowing us to reconnect with the world of senses and away from unhelpful thoughts.

Narrative coaching approach is a mindful, experiential and holistic approach to helping people shift their stories about themselves, about others and about life itself to create results that matter to them.

Non-cognitive methods are processes of acquiring knowledge through the senses, experience or reasoning.

Reframing is a technique to help create a different way of looking at a situation, person or relationship by changing its meaning. The essential idea behind reframing is that a person's point of view depends on the frame it is viewed in. When the frame is shifted, the meaning changes, and thinking and behaviour often change along with it.

Sensory engagement is engaging with our senses from looking, hearing, touching, feeling and tasting, to get involved emotionally and foster a sense of connectedness.

Storytelling is an interactive way of using words and actions to reveal the elements and images of a story while encouraging the listener's imagination.

References

Adler, N.J. (2006). The arts and leadership: Now that we can do anything, what will we do? *Academy of Management Learning and Education,* 5(4), pp. 486–499.

Adler, N.J. (2011). Leading beautifully: The creative economy and beyond. *Journal of Management Inquiry,* 20(3), pp. 208–221.

Adsera, A. (2004). Changing fertility rates in developed countries. The impact of labor market institutions. *Journal of Population Economics,* 17(1), pp. 17–43.

Alston, M. (2014). Gender mainstreaming and climate change. *Women's Studies International Forum,* 47(part B), pp. 287–297.

Amanatullah, E.T. and Morris, M.W. (2010). Negotiating gender roles: Gender differences in assertive negotiating are mediated by women's fear of backlash and attenuated when negotiating on behalf of others. *Journal of Personality and Social Psychology,* 98(2), pp. 256–267.

Ambady, N., Paik, S.K., Steele, J., Owen-Smith, A. and Mitchell, J.P. (2004). Deflecting negative self-relevant stereotype activation: The effects of individuation. *Journal of Experimental Social Psychology,* 40, pp. 401–408.

Annesley, M., Verni, K. and Dalziel, T. (2015). *Practical Mindfulness.* London: Dorling Kindersley Limited.

Aviv, V. (2014). *What does the brain tell us about abstract art?* Retrieved from: http://journal.frontiersin.org/article/10.3389/fnhum.2014.00085/full (Accessed: December 29, 2015).

Azmatullah, S. (2013). *The Coach's Mind Manual: Enhancing Coaching Practice with Neuroscience, Psychology and Mindfulness.* London: Taylor & Francis Group. Retrieved from: https://ebookcentral.proquest.com/lib/northumbria/detai;.action?docID=1434011

Bachkirova, T., Cox, E. and Clutterbuck, D. (2018). Introduction. In E. Cox, T. Bachkirova and D. Clutterbuck (Eds.). *The Complete Handbook of Coaching.* London: Sage. pp. 1–5.

Barnard, C.I. (1938). *The Functions of the Executive* (25th ed.). Cambridge, MA: Harvard University Press.

Bass, B.M., Avolio, B.J. and Atwater, L. (1996). The transformational and transactional leadership of men and women. *Applied Psychology: An International Review,* 45(1), pp. 5–34.

Bear, S., Rahman, N. and Post, C. (2010). The impact of board diversity and gender composition on corporate social responsibility and firm reputation. *Journal of Business Ethics,* 97, pp. 207–221.

Benschop, Y., Mills, J.H., Mills, A. and Tienari, J. (2012). Editorial: Gendering change: The next step. *Gender, Work and Organization,* 19(1), pp. 1–9.

Berkery, E., Morley, M. and Tiernan, S. (2013). Beyond gender role stereotypes and requisite managerial characteristics. From communal to androgynous, the changing views of women. *Gender in Management: An International Journal,* 28(5), pp. 278–298.

Boje, D.M. (1999). *Narrative Therapy.* Retrieved from: https://web.mnsu.edu/ (Accessed: November 15, 2021).

Brannen, J. and Nilsen, A. (2011). Comparative biographies in case-based cross-national research: Methodological considerations. *Sociology,* 45(4), pp. 603–618.

Brescoll, V.L. (2016). Leading with their hearts? How gender stereotypes of emotion lead to biased evaluations of female leaders. *The Leadership Quarterly,* 27, pp. 415–428.

Cassell, C. and Symon, G. (1994). *Qualitative Methods in Organizational Research. A Practical Guide.* London: Sage.

Cavanagh, M.J. and Spence, G.B. (2013). Mindfulness in coaching: Philosophy, psychology or just a useful skill? In J. Passmore, D.B. Peterson and T. Freire (Eds.). *Wiley-Blackwell Handbooks in Organizational Psychology. The Wiley-Blackwell Handbook of the Psychology of Coaching and Mentoring.* Hoboken, NJ: Wiley-Blackwell. pp. 112–134.

Chaskalson, M. & McMordie, M. (2018). *Mindfulness for Coaches. An Experimental Guide.* New York, NY: Routledge.

Cheryan, S., Plaut, V.C., Davies, P.G. and Steele, C.M. (2009). Ambient belonging: How stereotypical cues impact gender participation in computer science. *Journal of Personality and Social Psychology,* 97(6), pp. 1045–1060.

Child, J. (1997). Strategic choice in the analysis of action, structure, organizations and environment: Retrospect and prospect. *Organization Studies,* 18(1), pp. 43–76.

Chin, J.L. and Sanchez-Hucles, J. (2007). Diversity and leadership. *American Psychologist,* September 2007, pp. 608–609.

Christensen, C.M., McDonald, R., Altman, E.J. and Palmer, J.E. (2018). Disruptive innovation: An intellectual history and directions for future research. *Journal of Management Studies,* 55(7), pp. 1043–1078.

Ciesielska, M. and Jemielniak, D. (Eds.). (2018). *Qualitative Research in Organization Studies: Volume 1: Theories and New Approaches.* London: Palgrave Macmillan.

Ciesielska, M., Wolanik Boström, K. and Öhlander, M. (2018). Observational research. In M. Ciesielska and D. Jemielniak (Eds.). *Qualitative Research in Organization Studies: Volume 2: Methods and Possibilities.* London: Palgrave Macmillan. pp. 33–52.

CIPD. (2015). Learning and development. Retrieved from: www.cipd.co.uk/ Images/learning-development_2015_tcm18-11298.pdf (Accessed: December 28, 2020).

Clinton, H. (2010). Be pretty, but not too pretty: Why women just can't win. C. Rampell. Retrieved from: www.washingtonpost.com/opinions/no-women-still-cant-win-in-politics-and-business/2016/01/21/5529c28e-c079-11e5-83d4-42e3bceea902_story.html (Accessed: November 2, 2020).

Coe, C., Zehender, A. and Kinkew, D. (2008). *Coaching for Commitment: Achieving Superior Performance from Individuals and Teams* (3rd ed.). San Francisco, CA: Chichester Jossey-Bass; John Wiley.

Cohen, G.L., Garcia, J., Apfel, N. and Master, A. (2006). Reducing the racial achievement gap: A social-psychological intervention. *Science*, 313, pp. 1307–1310.

Cole, G.A. and Kelly, P. (2015). *Management Theory and Practice*. Boston: Cengage Learning.

Cunliffe, A.L. (2002). Reflexive dialogical practice in management learning. *Management Learning*, 33(1), pp. 35–61.

Cunliffe, A.L. (2004). On becoming a critically reflexive practitioner. *Journal of Management Education*, 28(4), pp. 407–426.

Cunliffe, A.L. (2009a). *A very short, fairly interesting and reasonably cheap book about management*. London: Sage.

Cunliffe, A.L. (2009b). Reflexivity, learning and reflexive practice. In S.J. Armstrong and C.V. Fukami (Eds.). *The Sage Handbook of Management, Learning, Education and Development*. London: Sage.

Cunliffe, A.L. and Easterby-Smith, M. (2004). From reflection to practical reflexivity: Experiential learning as lived experience. In M. Reynolds and R. Vince (Eds.). *Organizing Reflection*. Aldershot: Ashgate Publishing Ltd.

Cunningham, G.B., Bergman, M.E. and Miner, K.N. (2014). Interpersonal mistreatment of women in the workplace. *Sex Roles: A Journal of Research*, 71(1–2), pp. 1–6.

Cureton, P. and Stewart, J. (2014). *Designing, Delivering and Evaluating Learning and Development: Essentials in Practice*. London: Chartered Institute of Personnel and Development.

Davids, T., van Driel, F. and Parren, F. (2014). Feminist Change Revisited: Gender Mainstreaming As Slow Revolution. *Journal of Internal Development*, 26, pp. 396–408.

Davies, P.G., Spencer, S.J. and Steele, C.M. (2005). Clearing the air: Identity safety moderates the effects of stereotype threat on women's leadership aspirations. *Journal of Personality and Social Psychology*, 88(2), pp. 276–287.

Derks, B., van Laar, C. and Ellemers, N. (2016). The queen bee phenomenon: Why women leaders distance themselves from junior women. *The Leadership Quarterly*, 27, pp. 456–469.

de Vries, J.A. (2015). Champions of gender equality: Female and male executives as leaders of gender change. *Equality, Diversity and Inclusion: An International Journal*, 34(1), pp. 21–36.

de Waal, M. (2006). Evaluating gender mainstreaming in development projects. *Development in Practice*, 16(2), pp. 209–214.

Dobbin, F. and Kalev, A. (2013). The origins and effects of corporate diversity programs. In Q.M. Roberson (Ed.). *Oxford Handbook of Diversity at Work*. Oxford: Oxford University Press.

Drake, D. (2018). Narrative coaching. In E. Cox, T. Bachkirova and D. Clutterbuck (Eds.). *The Complete Handbook of Coaching*. London: Sage. pp. 109–123.

du Toit, A. (2014). *Making Sense of Coaching*. London: Sage.

Eagly, A.H. (1987). *Sex Differences in Social Behaviour: A Social-Role Interpretation*. London: Lawrence Erlbaum Associates.

Eagly, A.H. and Carli, L.L. (2007). *Through the Labyrinth: The Truth About How Women Become Leaders*. Boston, MA: Harvard Business School Press.

Eagly, A.H. and Chin, J.L. (2010). Diversity and leadership in a changing world. *American Psychologist*, 65(3), pp. 216–224.

Eagly, A.H. and Heilman, M.E. (2016). Gender and leadership: Introduction to the special issue. *The Leadership Quarterly*, 27, pp. 349–353.

Eagly, A.H. and Johannesen-Schmidt, M.C. (2001). The leadership styles of women and men. *Journal of Social Issues*, 57(4), pp. 781–797.

Eagly, A.H. and Karau, S.J. (2002). Role congruity theory of prejudice toward female leaders. *Psychological Review*, 109(3), pp. 573–598.

Eagly, A.H. and Wood, W. (1999). The origins of sex differences in human behaviour. Evolved dispositions versus social roles. *American Psychologist*, 54(6), pp. 408–423.

Edwards, G., Elliott, C., Iszatt-White, M. and Schedlitzki, D. (2013). Creative and alternative approaches to leadership learning. *Management Learning*, 44(1), pp. 3–10.

Eisner, E.W. (2004). What can education learn from the arts about the practice of education? *International Journal of Education and the Arts*, 5(4), pp. 1–13.

Ely, R.J., Ibarra, H. and Kolb, D.M. (2011). Taking gender into account: Theory and design for women's leadership development programs. *Academy of Management Learning and Education*, 10(3), pp. 474–493.

European Commission. (2016). Gender balance on corporate boards – Europe is cracking the glass ceiling. Retrieved from: www.ec.europa.eu/newsroom/document.cfm?doc_id.46280 (Accessed: March 27, 2018).

Fitzsimmons, T.W. and Callan, V.J. (2016). Applying a capital perspective to explain continued gender inequality in the C-suite. *The Leadership Quarterly*, 27, pp. 354–370.

Flaherty, J. (2010). *Coaching: Evoking Excellence in Others* (3rd ed.). Amsterdam: Elsevier, Butterworth-Heinemann.

Gay, P. (1994). *As She Likes It: Shakespeare's Unruly Women*. London: Routledge.

Gold, J., Holden, R., Iles, P., Stewart, J. and Beardwell, J. (2013). *Human Resource Development: Theory and Practice*. Basingstoke: Palgrave Macmillan.

Gray, D.E. (2007). Facilitating management learning. Developing critical reflection through reflective tools. *Management Learning*, 38(5), pp. 495–517.

Gray, D.E. (2009). *Doing Research in the Real World* (2nd ed.). London: Sage.

Guillaume, C. and Pochic, S., (2009). What would you sacrifice? Access to top management and the work-life balance. *Gender, Work and Organization,* 16(1), pp. 14–36.

Hall, L. (2015). Mindful coaching. How mindfulness can transform coaching practice. London: Kogan Page.

Hampton-Alexander Review. (2019). FTSE women leaders. Retrieved from: https://ftsewomenleaders.com/wp-content/uploads/2019/11/HA-Review-Report-2019.pdf

Hansen, H., Ropo, A. and Sauer, E. (2007). Aesthetic leadership. *The Leadership Quarterly,* 18(6), pp. 544–560.

Hawkins, P. and Smith, N. (2006). *Coaching, Mentoring and Organisational Consultancy.* London: Open University Press.

Haynes, M.C. and Heilman, M.E. (2013). It had to be you (not me)! Women's attributional rationalization of their contribution to successful joint work outcomes. *Personality and Social Psychology Bulletin,* 39(7), pp. 956–969.

Heilman, M.E. (2012). Gender stereotypes and workplace bias. *Research in Organizational Behaviour,* 32, pp. 113–135.

Heilman, M.E. and Okimoto, T.G. (2007). Why are women penalized for success at male tasks? The implied communality deficit. *Journal of Applied Psychology,* 92(1), pp. 81–92.

Holt, R. and Macpherson, A. (2010). Sensemaking, rhetoric and the socially competent entrepreneur. *International Small Business Journal,* 28(1), pp. 20–42.

Homer, K. (2019). Following in the footsteps of Aristotle and Steve Jobs – Five benefits of coaching whilst walking. Retrieved from: www.linkedin.com/pulse/following-footsteps-aristotle-steve-jobs-five-benefits-homer-/ (Accessed: August 27, 2020).

House of Commons Library. (2018). Women and the economy. Retrieved from: http://parliament.uk/commons-library (Accessed: March 30, 2018).

House of Commons Library. (2020). Women and the economy. Briefing Paper Number: CBP06838. Retrieved from: file:///C:/Users/nypg5/Dropbox/My%20PC%20(C20501548)/Downloads/SN06838%20(2).pdf

Hoyt, C.L. and Blascovich, J. (2010). The role of leadership self-efficacy and stereotype activation on cardiovascular, behavioral and self-report responses in the leadership domain. *The Leadership Quarterly,* 21, pp. 89–103.

Hoyt, C.L. and Murphy, S.E. (2016). Managing to clear the air: Stereotype threat, women, and leadership. *The Leadership Quarterly,* 27, pp. 387–399.

Hunt, C.M. and Fielden, S.L. (2016). *Coaching for Women Entrepreneurs. New Horizons in Management Series.* Cheltenham: Edward Elgar.

Hurn, B.J. (2013). Are cracks now appearing in the boardroom glass ceiling? *Industrial and Commercial Training,* 45(4), pp. 195–201.

Ibarra, H. (1993). Personal networks of women and minorities in management: A conceptual framework. *Academy of Management Review,* 18(1), pp. 56–87.

Ibarra, H. and Barbulescu, R. (2010). Identity as narrative prevalence, effectiveness, and consequences of narrative identity work in macro work role transitions. *Academy of Management Review,* 35(1), pp. 135–165.

Institute for Fiscal Studies. (2018). The rise and rise of women's employment in the UK. IFS Briefing Note BN234. Retrieved from: www.ifs.org.uk/uploads/BN234.pdf.art and literature (Accessed: 3 December, 2020).

Jung, C.G. (1966). *On the Relation of Analytical Psychology to Poetry. The Spirit in Man, Art and Literature.* Princeton: Princeton University Press. pp. 65–83.

Kalinoski, Z.T., Steele-Johnson, D., Peyton, E.J., Leas, K.A., Steinke, J. and Bowling, N.A. (2013). A meta-analytic evaluation of diversity training outcomes. *Journal of Organizational Behaviour*, 34, pp. 1076–1104.

Kanter, R.M. (1977). *Men and Women of the Corporation.* New York: Basic Books.

Kauffman, C., Boniwell, I. and Silberman, J. (2010). the positive psychology approach to coaching. In E. Cox, T. Bachkirova and D. Clutterbuck (Eds.). *The Complete Handbook of Coaching.* London: Sage. pp. 158–171.

Kelan, E.K. and Dunkley Jones, R. (2010). Gender and the MBA. *Academy of Management Learning and Education*, 9(1), pp. 26–43.

King, N., Brooks, J. and Tabari, S. (2018). Template analysis in business and management research. In M. Ciesielska and D. Jemielniak (Eds.). *Qualitative Methodologies in Organization Studies. Volume 11: Methods and Possibilities.* Switzerland: Springer Nature.

Koivunen, N. and Wennes, G. (2011). Show us the sound! Aesthetic leadership of symphony orchestra conductors. *Leadership*, 7(1), pp. 51–71.

Kolb, A.Y. and Kolb, D.A. (2008). Experiential learning theory: A dynamic, holistic approach to management learning, education and development. In S.J. Armstrong and C. Fukami (Eds.). *Handbook of Management Learning, Education and Development.* London: Sage.

Kostera, M. (2008). *Organizational Epics and Sagas.* London: Palgrave Macmillan.

Kumra, S. and Vinnicombe, S. (2008). A study of the promotion of partner process in a professional services firm: How women are disadvantaged. *British Journal of Management*, 19, pp. S65–S74.

Ladkin, D. and Taylor, S.S. (2010). Enacting the 'true self': Towards a theory of embodied authentic leadership. *The Leadership Quarterly,* 21(1), pp. 64–74.

Lakoff, G. and Johnson, M. (1980). *Metaphors We Live By.* Chicago: University of Chicago Press.

Lee, G. & Roberts, I. (2010). Coaching for authentic leadership. In J. Passmore (Ed.). *Leadership Coaching.* London: Kogan Page.

Lee-Gosselin, H., Briere, S. and Hawo, A. (2013). Resistances to gender mainstreaming in organizations: Toward a new approach. *Gender in Management: An International Journal*, 28(8), pp. 468–485.

Lee, R.M. (2000). *Unobtrusive Methods in Social Research.* Buckingham: Open University Press.

Lippa, R.A. (2005). *Gender, Nature and Nurture* (2nd ed.). London: Lawrence Erlbaum Associates.

Lombardo, E. and Mergaert, L. (2013). Gender mainstreaming and resistance to gender training: A framework for studying implementation. *Nordic Journal of Feminist and Gender Research*, 21(4), pp. 296–311.

Mahapatro, M. (2014). Mainstreaming gender. Shifts from advocacy to policy. *Vision*, 18(4), pp. 309–315.

Marcus, R. and Harper, C. (2014). *Gender Justice and Social Norms – Processes of Char for Adolescent Girls*. London: Overseas Development Institute. Retrieved from: www.odi.org/sites/odi.org.uk/files/odi-assets/publications-opinion-files/8831.pdf (Accessed: December 21, 2014).

McGaugh, J.L., Introini-Collison, I.B., Nagahara, A.H., Cahill, L., Brioni, J.D. and Castellano, C. (1990). Involvement of the amygdaloid complex in neuromodulatory influences on memory storage. *Neuroscience and Biobehavioral Review*, 14(4), pp. 425–431.

McGowan, P., Redeker, C.L., Cooper, S.Y. and Greenan, K. (2012). Female entrepreneurship and the management of business and domestic roles: Motivations, expectations and realities. *Entrepreneurship and Regional Development*, 24(1–2), pp. 53–72.

McNiff, S. (1981). *The Arts and Psychotherapy*. Springfield, IL: Charles C. Thomas.

Morgan, G. (2006). *Images of Organization*. London: Sage.

Mukhopadhyay, M. (2014). Mainstreaming gender or reconstituting the mainstream? Gender knowledge in development. *Journal of International Development*, 26, pp. 356–367.

Mukhopadhyay, M., Steehouwer, G. and Wong, F. (2006). Politics of the possible. Gender mainstreaming and organisational change: Experiences from the field. Retrieved from: www.kit.nl/gender/wp-content/uploads/publications (Accessed: March 20, 2017).

OECD. (2011). The future of families to 2030. A synthesis report. Retrieved from: www.oecd.org/futures/49093502.pdf (Accessed: February 10, 2020).

Office for National Statistics. (2010). Standard occupational classification. Retrieved from: http://ons.gov.uk (Accessed: May 11, 2018).

Office for National Statistics. (2018a). *Understanding the gender pay gap in the UK*. Retrieved from: www.ons.gov.uk (Accessed: May 1, 2018).

Office for National Statistics. (2018b). *Contracts that do not guarantee a minimum number of hours*. Retrieved from: www.ons.gov.uk (Accessed: May 11, 2018).

Office for National Statistics. (2020). Home employment and labour market people in work. Retrieved from: www.ons.gov.uk/employmentandlabourmarket/peopleinwork (Accessed: March 23, 2021).

Olivier, R. and Verity, J. (2008). Rehearsing tomorrow's leaders: The potential of 'mythodrama'. *Business Strategy Series*, 9(3), pp. 138–143.

Owen Blakemore, J.E. and Hill, C.A. (2008). The child gender socialization scale: A measure to compare traditional and feminist parents. *Sex Roles: A Journal of Research*, 58(3–4), pp. 192–207.

Pallier, G. (2003). Gender differences in the self-assessment of accuracy on cognitive tasks. *Sex Roles: A Journal of Research*, 48(5/6), pp. 265–276.

Palmer, S. and Whybrow, A. (Eds). (2019). *Handbook of Coaching Psychology: A Guide for Practitioners*. London: Taylor & Francis Group.

Parkin, M. (2003, 2010). *Tales for Coaching. Using Stories and Metaphors with Individuals and Small Groups*. London: Kogan Page.

Parpart, J.L. (2014). Exploring the transformative potential of gender mainstreaming in international development institutions. *Journal of International Development*, 26, pp. 382–395.

Passmore, J. (2010). A grounded theory study of the coachee experience: The implications for training and practice in coaching psychology. *International Coaching Psychology Review*, 5(1), pp. 48–62.

Passmore, J., Peterson, D.B., Freire, T. (2012). *The Wiley-Blackwell Handbook of the Psychology of Coaching and Mentoring*. Hoboken, NJ: John Wiley & Sons.

Patton, M.Q. (2002).*Qualitative Research and Evaluation Methods* (3rd ed.). Newbury Park, CA: Sage.

Perrault, E. (2015). Why does board gender diversity matter and how do we get there? The role of shareholder activism in deinstitutionalizing old boys' networks. *Journal of Business Ethics*, 128, pp. 149–165.

Phelan, J.E., Moss-Racusin, C.A. and Rudman, L.A. (2008). Competent yet out in the cold: Shifting criteria for hiring reflect backlash toward agentic women. *Psychology of Women Quarterly*, 32, pp. 406–413.

Phelan, J.E. and Rudman, L.A. (2010). Prejudice toward female leaders: Backlash effects and women's impression management dilemma. *Social and Personality Psychology Compass*, 4(10), pp. 807–820.

Powell, G.N. (1999). *Handbook of Gender and Work*: *Reflections on the Glass Ceiling*. Newbury Park, CA: Sage.

Purser, R. (2019). The mindfulness conspiracy. *The Guardian*, June 14, 2019. Retrieved from: www.theguardian.com/lifeandstyle/2019/jun/14/the-mindfulness-conspiracy-capitalist-spirituality (Accessed: November 31, 2020).

Purvis, B., Mao, Y. and Robinson, D. (2018). Three pillars of sustainability: In search of conceptual origins. *Sustainability Science*, 14, pp. 681–695. https://doi.org/10.1007/s11625-018-0627-5(012)

Roberts, L.M. and Creary, S.J. (2013). Navigating the Self in Diverse Work Contexts. In Q.M. Roberson (Ed.). *Oxford Handbook of Diversity and Work*. Oxford: Oxford University Press.

Rosenthal, H.E.S., Crisp, R.J. and Suen, M.W. (2007). Improving performance expectancies in stereotypic domains: Task relevance and the reduction of stereotype threat. *European Journal of Social Psychology*, 37, pp. 586–597.

Rowland, A.A., Dounas-Frazer, D.R., Ríos L., Lewandowski, H.J., Corwin, L.A. (2019). Using the life grid interview technique in stem educational research. *International Journal of STEM Education*, 6(1), pp. 1–13.

Rudman, L.A. and Glick, P. (2001). Prescriptive gender stereotypes and backlash toward agentic women. *Journal of Social Issues*, 57(4), pp. 743–762.

Ryan, M.K., Haslam, S.A., Morgenroth, T., Rink, F., Stoker, J. and Peters, K. (2016). Getting on top of the glass cliff: Reviewing a decade of evidence, explanations, and impact. *The Leadership Quarterly*, 27, pp. 446–455.

Saunders, N., Lewis, P. and Thornhill, A. (2012). *Research Methods for Business Students* (6th ed.). Essex: Pearson Education Ltd.

Scharmer, O. (2007). *Theory U: Leading from the Future as It Emerges.* Cambridge, MA: Society for Organisational Learning.

Schein, V.E. (1973). The relationship between sex role stereotypes and requisite management characteristics. *Journal of Applied Psychology,* 57(2), pp. 95–100.

Seo, G., Huang, W. and Han, S. (2017). Conceptual review of underrepresentation of women in senior leadership positions from a perspective of gendered social status in the workplace: Implication for HRD research and practice. Retrieved from: https://doi.or/10.1177/15344484317690063 (Accessed: November 14, 2020).

Seeley, C. and Reason, P. (2008). Expressions of energy: An epistemology of presentational knowing. In P. Liamputtong and J. Rumbold (Eds.). *Knowing Differently: Art-based and Collaborative Research.* New York: Nova Science Publishers.

Senge, P.M. (1990). *The Fifth Discipline. The art and practice of the learning organization.* New York: Doubleday/Currency.

Senge, P. (2006). *The Fifth Discipline: The Art and Practice of the Learning Organization.* New York: Doubleday.

Shapiro, J.R. and Neuberg, S.L. (2007). From stereotype threat to stereotype threats: Implications of a multi-threat framework for causes, moderators, mediators, consequences and interventions. *Society for Personality and Social Psychology*, 11(2), pp. 107–130.

Shields, S.A. (2002). *Speaking from the heart: Gender and the social meaning of emotion.* Cambridge: Cambridge University Press.

Shinar, E.H. (1975). Sexual stereotypes of occupations. *Journal of Vocational Behaviour*, 7, pp. 99–111.

Singh, V., Vinnicombe, S. and Kumra, S. (2006). Women in formal corporate networks: An organisational citizenship perspective. *Women in Management Review*, 21(6), pp. 458–482

Snow, D.A. and Anderson, L. (1987). Identity work among the homeless: The verbal construction and avowal of personal identities. *American Journal of Sociology*, 92(6), pp. 1336–1371.

Spencer, S.J., Steele, C.M. and Quinn, D.M. (1999). Stereotype threat and women's math performance. *Journal of Experimental Social Psychology*, 35(4), pp. 4–28.

Springborg, C. (2010). Leadership as art – Leaders coming to their senses. *Leadership,* 6(3), pp. 243–258.

Springborg, C. and Ladkin, D. (2018). Realising the potential of art-based interventions in managerial learning: Embodied cognition as an explanatory theory. *Journal of Business Research*, 85, pp. 532–539.

Springborg, C. and Sutherland, I. (2015). Teaching MBAs aesthetic agency through dance. *Organizational Aesthetics*, 5(1), pp. 94–113.

Steele, C.M. (1997). A threat in the air. How stereotypes shape intellectual identity and performance. *American Psychologist*, 52(6), pp. 613–629.

Steele, C.M. (2010). *Whistling Vivaldi and other clues to how stereotypes affect us.* New York: Norton.

Steele, C.M. and Aronson, J. (1995). Stereotype threat and the intellectual test performance of African Americans. *Journal of Personality and Social Psychology*, 69(5), pp. 797–811.

Steele, C.M., Spencer, S.J. and Aronson, J. (2002). Contending with group image: The psychology of stereotype and social identity threat. *Advances in Experimental Social Psychology*, 34, pp. 379–440.

Stelter, R. (2013). *A Guide to Third Generation Coaching: Narrative-Collaborative Theory and Practice*. New York: Springer Science.

Sutherland, I. (2012). Arts-based methods in leadership development: Affording aesthetic workspaces, reflexivity and memories with momentum. *Management Learning*, 44(1), pp. 25–43.

Sutherland, I. and Jelinek, J. (2015). From experiential learning to aesthetic knowing: The arts in leadership development. *Advances in Developing Human Resources*, 17(3), pp. 289–306.

Sveningsson, S. and Alvesson, M. (2003). Managing managerial identities: Organizational fragmentation, discourse and identity struggle. *Human Relations*, 56(10), pp. 1163–1193.

Taylor, S.S. and Ladkin, D. (2009). Understanding arts-based methods in managerial development. *Academy of Management Learning & Education*, 8(1), pp. 55–69.

Terjesen, S., Aguilera, R.V. and Lorenz, R. (2014). Legislating a women's seat on the board: Institutional factors driving gender quotas for boards of directors. *Journal of Business Ethics*, 128, pp. 233–251.

Thebaud, S. (2015). Business as plan b: Institutional foundations of gender inequality in entrepreneurship across 24 industrialized countries. *Administrative Science Quarterly*, 60(4), pp. 1–41.

Torrington, D., Hall, L., Taylor, S., Atkinson, C. (2009). *Fundamentals of Human Resource Management: Managing People at Work*. Harlow: Financial Times Prentice Hall.

van Eerdewijk, A. and Davids, T. (2014). Escaping the mythical beast: Gender mainstreaming reconceptualised. *Journal of International Development*, 26, pp. 303–316.

Varghese, L., Lindeman, M.I.H. and Finkelstein, L. (2018). Dodging the double bind: The role of warmth and competence on the relationship between interview communication styles and perceptions of women's hire ability. *European Journal of Work and Organizational Psychology*, 27(4), pp. 418–429.

Vinnicombe, S., Doldor, E., Sealy, R., Pryce, P. and Turner, C. (2015). The female FTSE board report 2015. Putting the U.K. progress in a global perspective. Retrieved from: http://som.cranfield.ac.uk/som/...ftse/femaleFTSEReportMarch2015.pdf (Accessed: June 25, 2015).

von Hippel., C., Issa, M., Ma, R. and Stokes, A. (2011). Stereotype threat: Antecedents and consequences for working women. *European Journal of Social Psychology*, 41, pp. 151–161.

Walker, E., Wang, C. and Redmond, J. (2008). Women and work-life balance: Is home-based business ownership the solution? *Equal Opportunities International*, 27(3), pp. 258–275.

Watson, T. (2015). The social sector's glass ceiling: Why women in leadership jobs matter. Retrieved from: http://forbes.com/sites/tomwatson/2015/01/30/the-social-sectors-glass-ceiling-why-women-in-leadership-jobs-matter (Accessed: February 1, 2015).

Weick, K.E. (1998). Introductory essay: Improvisation as a mindset for organizational analysis. *Organization Science*, 9(5), pp. 543–555.

Weick, K.E. (2006). Faith, evidence and action: Better guesses in an unknowable world. *Organization Studies,* 27(11), pp. 1723–1736.

Weick, K.E. (2007). Drop your tools: On reconfiguring management education. *Journal of Management Education,* 31(1), pp. 5–16.

Weick, K.E., Sutcliffe, K.M. and Obstfeld, D. (2005). Organizing and the process of sensemaking. *Organization Science,* 16(4), pp. 409–421.

Wheeler, S.C., DeMarree, K.G. and Petty, R.E. (2007). Understanding the role of the self in prime-to-behavior effects: The active-self account. *Society for Personality and Social Psychology*, 11(3), pp. 234–261.

Whitmore, J. (2017). *Coaching for Performance: The Principles and Practice of Coaching and Leadership* (5th ed.). New York: Nicholas Brearley Publishing.

Wicks, P.G. and Rippin, A. (2010). Art as experience: An inquiry into art and leadership using dolls and doll-making. *Leadership*, 6(3), pp. 259–278.

Witkin, R.W. (2009). The aesthetic imperative of a rational-technical machinery: A study in organizational control through the design of artifacts. *Music and Arts in Action*, 2(1), pp. 56–68.

Index

aesthetic 5–6

arts 8, 30, 80–81, 87; arts-based coaching 75–76, 87–89; arts-based methods/interventions 1, 4–6, 9–10, 30, 50–51, 60, 71, 75, 77, 79–80, 87, 93, 95, 106, 109; arts -based theories 6–9; *As You Like It* 9, 53–56, 59

attribute 1, 31, 41, 43, 49; agentic 26, 30–32, 35–37, 41; communal 35–36, 41

backlash effect 31, 40

behaviour 49–50, 54–57, 60–63, 72, 80, 82, 94, 95, 100, 106–107; agentic 32, 35–40, 47, 49, 66; communal 26, 32, 35–41; assertive 26, 43; gendered 49, 55–56, 61–63, 82, 87, 89, 106; nurturing, stereotypical 48, 76, 87, 106; body scan 51–53, 85–86

burn-out 49

career 5, 10, 17, 24, 27–30, 49, 55–58, 65–66, 73, 79, 90–91, 94, 101–102, 105; advancement 5, 7, 9–10, 12, 17, 19–21, 24, 33–35, 38, 41, 49, 60, 66, 91, 99–101; aspirations 5, 22, 24, 27–29, 67, 99, 102; capital 29, 33–35; early 24, 30, 35, 42, 44, 65, 94, 99, 101–102, 105

caring responsibilities 2, 19, 21, 28, 101

change 1, 14–15, 18–20, 54–55, 71, 74, 76, 82–83, 87–88,

97, 105; behaviour 8, 23, 46–47, 52, 59, 62, 70, 84, 93, 99–100, 109; organisational 14–16, 18, 24, 36, 49, 104, 108; resistance 15–16, 23, 25, 65, 73; in the workplace 2–4, 17; policy 13–14

coach 80–82, 89

coaching 14, 75–89, 109

confidence 29, 35–36, 38, 42, 44, 51–52, 59, 66–69, 71, 73, 81, 90–93, 101, 105, 108; lack of 33, 65, 94

culture 4, 9, 25, 80–81, 94; male-dominated 9, 20, 30, 36, 40, 43, 47–48, 61, 88, 94–95, 98–101; organisational 15–18, 20, 22, 25, 35, 40, 43–47, 51–52, 56, 61, 95, 98, 103, 105

Cunliffe, A.L. 6, 8, 22, 25, 76

discourse 22, 25

discrimination 23, 33; tory behaviour 19; tory language 45

diversity 4, 14, 102 ; interventions 50; management 102; training 17–18

double bind syndrome, 5, 32

Eagly, A.H. 1, 5, 16, 26, 31, 33–35, 40–41

education 28–29, 43, 48, 91, 102; management 50

empathy 36, 76

employment 2, 11, 17, 25, 41–42, 47–48, 90; rates 2–3

Employment Protection Act 2

enactment 20, 22, 25, 47

environment 17, 26, 43–47, 57–58, 65, 78, 86, 91; gendered 1, 14, 76–77, 87, 102; learning 30, 49, 56–57, 66; male-dominated 11, 18, 38, 40, 44, 46, 48, 60, 62, 93–100; mixed gender 11; VUCA (volatile, uncertain, complex, ambiguous) 55, 59; women-dominated 11, 56
equality 1–4, 12–18, 22–23, 32, 60, 88, 97–98, 100
Equal Pay Act 2

female 19, 32, 37–38, 41, 44, 48; characteristics qualities 5, 30, 59; employment 2–4 talent 4; role model 102; stereotype 31, 40
feminine 24, 26, 31, 36, 40, 49, 94, 103–104
feminist 8, 15
flexible working policies 14, 19, 21, 79, 102
FTSE 4

gender 5, 9–16, 23–26, 44, 47, 54–59, 82, 97–98, 108; balance 4; differences 22, 24–25; downplaying 44–45; equality xvii, 1, 12–16, 18, 22, 97–98; inequality 4, 16; mainstreaming 12–15, 17–22, 24; norms 31, 49, 56; pay gap xvii, 3; role 15, 25–28, 31, 55; social construct 17, 24, 26, 47; stereotype 1, 5, 8, 10, 13, 17, 20, 23, 25–27, 29–43, 45–49, 57, 62, 66–67, 71–72, 75–77, 80–81, 83, 86–89, 99, 103–104, 106, 109; targets and quotas 17; training 14–15, 17
gendered: behaviours 4, 10, 14, 23–24, 27, 49, 56–57, 61, 63, 87, 89; beliefs 19, 45; work environment 76–78, 87, 102; roles 27–30, 55
glass cliff phenomenon 26
government 15, 21

Heilman, M.E. 1, 5, 26, 31, 33, 40
human 53, 77, 80, 82 : capital 34; resources 4, 89, 99, 101–103; resource development 14–17; resource managers 17, 36

identity 1, 9, 15, 22, 32–34, 47, 55, 76–77, 82, 85, 87–88; professional 69, 87
individualised approach xvii, 71, 75–76, 81–82, 87

Kanter, R.M. 32, 47–48

leader 1, 5, 16, 26, 31, 35, 48, 50, 59, 65; woman 5
leadership 5–6, 14, 16–17, 21, 25–27, 30–31, 33, 35–36, 47, 49, 54–56, 59, 65, 72, 76, 79–80, 88, 103; authentic 85; development 6, 8, 44, 51, 53, 85, 87; style 10, 24, 26, 31–32, 35, 38, 40–41, 49
learning 5–6, 8, 11, 14, 29–30, 71–72, 75, 78–79, 82–85; arts- based 1, 53–56, 82, 8–89; environment 49, 54, 66; self-developed 56, 59–61; style 50, 56–57
life-grid interview 9, 56, 82
lifestyle 21–22, 47, 101

manager 20, 38, 44, 60–61, 91, 94–95, 99–100, 105–106; female 44, 60, 95, 100, 105; HR 19; male 19, 31–32, 104–105
masculine 6, 24, 26, 30–33, 35, 37, 40, 48–49, 56, 88, 94, 96–97, 103–104
meditation 51, 53, 85–86
mental models 22, 25, 47
mentor 20, 89
mentoring 14, 34, 41, 48, 78–79, 89
metaphor 9, 20, 25, 27, 51–53, 55, 61, 65, 67, 71, 81–84, 93, 108–109; -ical engagement 51–52, 81, 87
mindfulness 81, 85–86, 109
Morgan, G. 20, 25
mythodrama 50, 53–54, 59

narrative 28, 36–38, 40, 44, 46, 65–66, 68, 71, 81–82, 100, 103, 109
normative expectations 25, 31, 40

Olivier R. 50, 53–54
organisational 4, 7–8, 1, 17, 20, 23, 25, 27, 33–34, 38 39, 41–42, 48,

57, 59, 75, 88, 105; change 14–16, 18, 24, 36, 49, 89, 100, 104, 108; champions 16, 18; credibility 4; contexts 16, 22, 26, 47, 82, 94; culture 15–18, 20, 22, 25, 35, 40, 43–47, 51–52, 56, 61, 89, 94–95, 98, 101, 103–105, 108; development 12, 15, 18, 53, 80, 101, 103; levels 11; performance 4; policies 12–14, 19

Passmore, J. 79–80, 83
photography 50, 71, 106
poetry 71, 106, 109
positive psychology 51, 79; in coaching 76–77, 79–81, 87
power xvi, 2, 15, 17, 23, 25–26, 32, 41, 43, 78, 80, 101, 106; blindness 16; relations 12, 16, 19, 104; inequality 19–20, 48; institutional 16
professional development 14, 79, 87–88; expertise 44, 73, 95; identity 69; integrity 106; networks 91; qualifications 29; women 23–24, 26–27, 32, 34, 42–43, 46–49, 75, 78, 80–82, 86–88
psychic prison 20, 25, 27
public: image 35, 47, 49; sector 18, 26, 66, 69, 98

queen bee syndrome 32

recruitment process 10, 13, 19–22, 98
reflection 49, 51–56, 59, 67, 72–73, 78, 81–82, 85, 100
reflexive practice 8–9, 56, 59
reframing 51–52, 59, 80–81, 83, 108–109
relaxation 51–53, 85
role models 4, 43, 102, 105

self 1, 7–10, 39, 54–55, 75–77, 85, 88, 95, 100; and others 7, 25, 29–30, 35, 55, 75–81; belief 21, 71–72, 81, 90–91; confidence 29, 33, 36, 42, 72, 93–94, 101, 105; control 61, 75, 108; doubt 29, 38–41, 49, 65, 71; efficacy 62, 67–70; protection

15, 19; reliance 37, 42; worth 62, 64–66, 108
sensemaking 7–8, 50–52, 56, 59, 63, 67, 72, 77, 81–85
sensory: engagement 59, 69, 71, 81, 85–86, 109; experience 7, 9, 50, 52, 57, 61–64, 67–68, 81, 87, 92, 96; words 51–52, 62, 70, 92
settledness 51–53, 72
Sex Discrimination Act 2
social 7–8, 15, 87; capital 33–34, 48; construction 20, 22–25, 47–48; network 10, 13, 34, 48, 102; norms 4, 24; participation 1–3, 17; role 26–28; work 105–106
socialisation 24
sponsor 20, 43–44
Springborg, C. 6–8, 51
Steele, C.M. 30, 32–33, 35 41, 46, 48, 109
stereotype: leader 31, 40–41; of a Northern woman 30; threat 1, 10, 29–30, 32–36, 41, 47–49, 57, 62, 67, 71–72, 77, 81, 86–89, 91, 99, 103–105, 109
sticky issue 54, 56, 73
storytelling 59, 81–82, 109
strategic choice theory 17, 19
Sutherland, I. 1, 5–8

tick box exercise 19, 21, 98–99
tokenism 18, 32, 47–48

United Nations 12

Verity, J. 50, 53

Weick, K.E. 6–8, 25, 53
Whitmore, J. 79–80
work 2, 9–10, 15, 17, 25–29, 33, 36–37, 42–43, 51–52, 57, 60, 66–67, 79, 86–88, 95, 100–103, 105–106; life 2, 5, 33–34, 55, 79, 85, 97
workshop 9–11, 21, 30, 38, 49–57, 59–74, 90, 92, 95, 97, 100, 103, 106–108

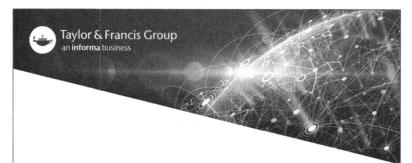

Printed in the United States
by Baker & Taylor Publisher Services